Poetry City, USA, Vol. 2

Poetry City, USA, Vol. 2

An anthology of poems read at the second annual Great Twin Cities Poetry Read + essays, interviews, reviews, and other prose on poetry

[Matt Mauch, orchestrator]

Lowbrow
Press

POETRY CITY, USA, VOL. 2
Copyright 2012

Cover design: Jeff Peterson

Published by Lowbrow Press
www.lowbrowpress.com

ISBN: 978-0-9829553-8-3

CONTENTS, TABLE OF

We are not a consumer group; we are a tribe
. . . our poems are what the gods couldn't
make without going through us.

— *Dean Young*

The second annual Great Twin Cities Poetry Read was held in the Fine Arts Theater at Normandale Community College on what will be recalled (whether or not it's true) as a lovely Friday, April 29, 2011.

Most of the poems found here were read there. Others were read at the GTCPR's standing Road Show home, The Maeve's Sessions. In addition to the poems you'll find reviews, interviews, essays, and other prose on poetry written by current and former participants and friends of the GTCPR + Road Show.

The GTCPR II was also a fundraiser for poet Dean Young's new heart.

More on Dean Young, the fundraising, the Great Twin Cities Poetry Read + Road Show, and The Maeve's Sessions can be found in the pages that follow. You can keep track of GTCPR + RS happenings throughout the year, and find information not presented here, at GreatTwinCitiesPoetryReadandRoadShow.com.

Turn the page.

My Friends the Twin Cities

Standing in front of the mic at last year's Great Twin Cities
Poetry Read, I was a wreck. I had just returned from visiting
Dean Young in Austin, Tex., where his heart was failing due to
idiopathic hypotropic cardiomyopathy. He had been hooked
up to a portable heart pump the size of a suitcase, and was
desperately awaiting a life-saving transplant.

When I returned from Austin, Matt Mauch immediately
offered up the GTCPR as an impromptu fundraiser for
Dean's National Foundation for Transplants fund. So after
scrambling with Matt — it's impossible to thank Matt
adequately here — to get things organized with the NFT and
our generous local sponsors, there I was, up at the mic, trying
to deliver the big fundraising pitch, wondering whether
everyone was thinking the same thing: *for the love of God,
please don't make me watch the Tall Man cry.*

My expectations, I'm embarrassed to admit now, were
modest. We're poets, not titans of industry, I thought.
We carry chapbooks, not checkbooks. Driving over to
Normandale College before the event, I decided I'd be happy
if we raised $200.

The outpouring of support for Dean was overwhelming.
The little wicker basket I had placed on the table by the door
overflowed with cash and checks. I don't mean to be crass;
I mean to be accurate. Very few people left that reading
without giving and giving generously. We raised more than
$1,000, not counting anyone who went online and donated
from home. This was, by the way, significantly more money
than was raised at a heavily promoted New York City
event, headlined by fancy poets in one of those places with
chancellors and chandeliers.

This Poetry City U.S.A. idea might not be entirely tongue in
cheek after all.

***

Dean and I have been friends since the mid-1990s, when I was a mediocre and misguided fiction student in the Indiana University MFA program. When Dean's then-wife, the novelist Cornelia Nixon, became my thesis advisor, we all became fast friends. Dean and Neal threw great parties. I just threw up.

In those days, in addition to walking around and being stupid, I was running a lot — even a marathon, which like my fiction, was performed without distinction. My friendship with Dean was built, in part, during long runs in the sweltering Indiana sun. Despite being 15 years my senoir, and having the stride of a misdeveloped ostrich, Dean would run me into the pavement. After a few miles I would be struggling to keep pace.

Knowing this, which is I hope not knowing too much, you can imagine how impossible it was to accept what I saw when I arrived at Dean and Laurie's house in Austin last April. In the abstract, I knew all about Dean's portable pump; the blood navigating the clear tubes in his bandaged chest; the stresses the surgery, medication, and wheezing machinery had placed on his body. At one point, thinking he wasn't going to make it though an emergency surgery, he told me — well, the things one says to a friend in those circumstances.

What's more memorable now, however, is the way Dean carried himself with such grace and courage while this was happening to him. About an hour into my visit, I decided it was time to try cracking a joke at his expense, and he shot one right back at me with topspin — in that familiar game of minor-insult tennis that heterosexual males play to express affection for one another. I remember feeling a tiny relief. It was hard to see how things were going to turn out okay for Dean, but he still had that Dean Fire, which is pure magic.

***

As I write this on the other side of the miracle — appropriately enough on New Year's Day 2012 — I'm thrilled to report that Dean is not only alive, he is triumphantly alive, a successful transplant survivor, a young man's heart beating away in his chest like a tom-tom. Last week he sent me a new poem and a weird sculpture he made out of a prosthetic eyeball and broken watchworks. He's trying to write again, and the letter said he thinks he's getting his mojo back. Prosthetic eyeballs and Superglue are good signs of mojo!

You should know how grateful Dean and Laurie are for your gift to his NFT fund. Dean's medical expenses will continue to challenge him, so if you're reading this and you haven't given, you can make a meaningful contribution here: http://www.transplants.org/donate/deanyoung.

What was amazing about last year's GTCPR was witnessing a full spectrum of poets in our community collectively take a stand on behalf of someone known widely to have dedicated his life to expanding the possibilities of our art form — Dean Young's great gift to us. How exciting to realize our friend Dean is about to sprint wildly ahead of us again, setting a new and more torrid pace.

COMATOSE

Pull me out of this wall,
spell me with letters traced on my back,
my thigh, my wrist, traced with fingertips
light as a daisy petal. Pull me out
of this plaster, this stasis, sing me out with rhymes
against the cartilage of my ears, loud as trumpets.
Pull me past the studs, the framing, conjugate
the verbs of my muscles, bend my arms until
they fold around your shoulders. Pull me from
behind the pipes and outlets, coax the words
from my throat as you would a butterfly
from its chrysalis, with slow, light presses
of the thumb, until the edge cracks, and
my first words emerge with wet wings,
fervent, trembling.

Brad Liening

"You Enter the Ballerina's Lair": An Appreciation of Dean Young

Dean Young has made my life infinitely richer. Dean's poetry alone is enough to distinguish him as a life-changer, a force of nature, one of those rare individuals who pushes an art form ahead with a great shove. We can all be grateful for his contributions to American letters.

I was also lucky enough to know Dean as a teacher several years ago, when I was in graduate school. He came along at a time when I felt enormously confused about poetry and, more generally, life, and he made an enormously positive impact. He was perceptive and honest and generous with his feedback; he clearly gave a lot of time and effort to his students in workshops, in seminars, and in individual conferences. The guy really cared about our education.

But there was something besides his perspicacity that was just as important to me that spring: he was fun. Dean injected humor and vitality into class and into poetry without sacrificing a jot of intelligence or rigor.

And oh, how I needed this.

I needed some sense of play and fun. I didn't know it at the time, but I was looking for someone to give me permission to totally and royally screw up.

Some might argue that I've taken this lesson too much to heart. And I very much doubt that Dean would say he granted me such license. But when he told me one afternoon, gently but firmly, that my poems were far too derivative of a certain writer and that I needed to try some new things, hell, to try anything, if I wanted out of the dead end where I was stuck... something big hit home.

I felt like I was being given a much-needed boost over a wall. I felt like I was being given license to experiment, to write poems in which I didn't know what I was doing, and it would also be okay to have a little bit of fun doing it.

This is what MFA programs are for, of course. But this is

the sort of glaringly obvious lesson that's easy to hear but very hard to actually learn. I know I was often afraid to look stupid and/or untalented in front of my very smart and very talented classmates. This timidity manifested itself in the poems I was writing—I wrote the same poem for years!

Dean, though, gave me a great shove forward. He helped me learn that obvious and crucial lesson, one I've happily been learning in different ways for years thereafter.

It's not surprising that Dean was the one to help me learn this particular thing. I can distinctly recall reading his poems for the first time as an undergraduate, totally shocked that someone could have this much fun writing poetry. Or, perhaps more accurately, that I could have this much fun reading poetry. Oh, the temerity of this kind of resourceful joy! Reading Dean was like getting smacked in the face with a rose. It was like going through a car wash, *sans* car. The sheer inventiveness of his language and images made me a believer in not just the primacy and importance of his imagination and idiom, but also, weirdly, in my own.

Dean didn't solve all my problems, of course, nor did he make me a flawless writer. But he responded to everything and everyone with a wide-open heart and mind that I still find inspiring. We need people like Dean around to help make our dim lives brighter.

Tim Nolan

LEAVING

If I were beside
a Chinese river in the 6th century
I would pick few words

Someone is going away
down the path
that someone may turn

Because we are 6th century
Chinese friends
we are sad to take leave

We have pet crickets
at home in elegant
little enameled boxes

If you can pay attention
to a pet cricket
leave-taking must be hard

When we next meet
it will be winter—
the snow on the mountain

The fast fire
in the black stove—
Can you believe

We are atop
this jade mountain again—
the cold river rushing through?

John Medeiros

One Sentence

I learned it all from first grade to fifth when I learned the
components of a sentence, when I learned that the beauty of
language is that we are all part of that language, that as we
study what it means to be a noun, or a verb, or an adjective –
all things I will reveal later – we also, simultaneously, as if the
universes of emotion and alphabet were suddenly fused into
one, we also *feel* what it means to be a noun, or a verb, or an
adjective, and at that moment of fusion, when life becomes
the word on paper, I finally come to terms with my life: a
sentence, a line of words strung together sometimes with
meaning, sometimes without meaning, always containing
those things a sentence always seems to contain, like a noun,
a common noun at that, like *faggot* (as in *God hates a faggot*,
but not as in *God hates your faggot ways* because then I am
no longer a noun, but an adjective, and that, you will find,
comes much later in life), so instead my life, at this moment,
is a noun – sometimes a common noun but then sometimes
a proper noun (as in *Tommy*), or a compound noun (as in
twinship), or a collective noun (as in *the genes that made us
this way*), or a possessive noun (as in *I am and I will always
be, my brother's keeper*); and only once I am a noun, whether
it be a common noun or a proper noun or a collective noun
or a possessive noun – something inside me yearns to
be, something inside yearns to give the nouns in my life
meaning, and it is only when the desire to be burns inside
like an ember struggling to stay lit do I suddenly unfold and
become a verb – an inactive verb today (to be, as in *I am
gay*), an active verb tomorrow, as in *replicate* (like carbon
copies, or identical twins, or infectious viral particles); and
as a verb I will be a variety of tenses, sometimes more than
one simultaneously, sometimes just present (*I have AIDS*),
sometimes present continuous (*I am trying to tell you I have
AIDS*), sometimes just past (*I tried to tell you I have AIDS*), and
sometimes future (*I will die with this disease*); regardless of

which, I can be one or I can be all, but I will always be tense, and once I've seen myself as noun and verb I will slowly grow into adjective to describe myself and make myself more interesting to you, my audience, so that you will no longer see me as *your twin* but instead will come to know me as *your gay HIV-positive twin*, and to the parents who once knew me as *their son* I will be remembered as *their sick son*, sick from too much language and too much love, adjectives can do that to a person, and sometimes the adjective I become is multiple in meaning, and so I am split (as in *zygote*) and split (as in *personality*) – the adjectives I become can be confusing to a person; the adverb, on the other hand, disassociates itself from the subject and marries itself instead to its action; so, whereas I love, I can now love too *deeply*, and whereas I cry, I now cry *passionately*, and when it comes to loving, and when it comes to crying the sentence of my life takes on objects, and when those objects are direct I no longer love too deeply, instead I love *you* too deeply, and when those objects are indirect I no longer cry passionately, I cry passionately only *for you*, and so it is, as is the case with most twins, that the components of my life take on meaning and structure, and my life becomes the very sentence I use to describe it; yet like a sentence, as in the string of words full of subject and predicate, my life, too, is another sentence, a prison sentence, as in removed from the outside world, a sentence as in a final verdict, a judgment, a lack of freedom, or a loss of freedom once owned, a life once held in the palm of my hand and then taken away, forever, leaving me with only a series of words never without a verb to follow; otherwise, if I could, I'd be *individual* or *asexual* or *undetectable*: words all by themselves – words, ironically, only befitting a prisoner.

Cullen Bailey Burns

PILGRIM

I shake his ashes from my hand.
The new world waits.

Oily they are, and coarse. One more state
in which to lie, to go forth from.

I have clutched at the transformation, licked
it from my fingers, the closest

I venture to belief. The modern mind can't help
its modern doubt. But here

he falls into pine needles beneath
the world of thought. Fair shore,

fair moon for setting out, fair moment
arriving. Rise.

William Reichard

Leaving School(s)

We're living in an age of polarization. Who can deny it?
The Republicans won't work with the Democrats and the
Democrats won't work with the Republicans and the Tea
Partiers hate everyone, except themselves. In Minnesota, in
the summer of 2011, we watched our state government shut
down due to lack of cooperation, an unwillingness or inability
of any of our representatives to compromise or come to any
kind of consensus. It was shocking, but perhaps it shouldn't
have been. We've been watching this same game of chicken
being played out on a national scale since Barak Obama took
office. A democratic president and a republican legislature—it
seems this can't end well.

This "us" vs. "them" mentality is nothing new to
humankind. We've been playing out this game since we
crawled out of the primordial ooze. I've started to think
that, as a species, we tend to define ourselves based not on
what we are, but on what we are not. We look around and
say, "I'm not that" and "I'm not that" and "I'm not that" and
what is left, the negative space as my visual artist friends
would call it, becomes our frame, the outline that defines
us. This doesn't seem like a very healthy way to approach
self-definition, but it's what most of us do. We like clear-cut
answers, binary kinds of things: either A or B, 1 or 2, black or
white, right or wrong. Sometimes it feels like we're trapped
in a perpetual eye exam, with the doctor flipping the little
lenses back and forth, asking which is clearer, #1 or #2, #3 or
#4. Except, in this case, none of the lenses make our sense of
self or our world any clearer. There are just varying degrees of
blurriness.

So what has all of this got to do with poetry? Good
question. While I've been pondering the polarization within
our overall society, I've been considering the ways in which
this mentality spills over into specific points on our socio-
cultural map, and because I'm a poet (always by nature and

sometimes by trade) I've thought a lot about various factions or schools of contemporary poetry, why they exist, and what, if any, value they bring to the craft. I'm the product of a dual education. I have an MA in Creative Writing and a Ph.D. in American Literature. While I worked on my creative degree, I also worked on my academic degree, and like most messy humans, work from one project often spilled over into the other. In retrospect, I wouldn't have it any other way. I believe that the competing emphasis on the creative process and on critical analysis made me a better poet and a better thinker, a pragmatic dreamer, if you will.

It was in graduate school that I first encountered the differences between various "schools" of poetry. Early on, someone asked me what kind of work I wrote. I'd honestly never spent a lot of time trying to label my work, but since I tend to write short, lyric work that often contains elements of narrative, I replied, "I write lyric narrative poetry." My answer was met with silence, and then a very serious reply: "You can't be. You can write lyric poetry or you can write narrative poetry. They're two different things." My questioner huffed off, certain, I'm sure, that I was not the stuff of academic genius. I stood there, puzzled and slightly panicked. What *was* I, poetically speaking? Why didn't I know? Was I supposed to know? I don't recall answering that question on the GED.

Granted, in this story I'm really talking more about *styles* of poetry than *schools*, but the point is the same: Most people like to categorize, to name, identify, even own, if only in an intellectual, virtual way, what surrounds them. This urge, something I've come to call the taxonomic drive, is strong, and it absolutely flourishes in academic settings. After that initial experience, I started to pay more attention to what was happening around me, poetically and stylistically speaking. I recognized that, for some, their support of one style of poetry over another wasn't limited merely to what they liked or disliked, it was really about allegiances, their loyalty to one school of poetry over another. One of my teachers was deeply committed to the "deep image." Another was wrapped up in the work of the New York school. Another fascinated only by the work of the Bay Area poets of the '50s and '60s. In my own cohort of graduate program poets, there were some lyric narrative writers (impossible, I know, but let's go with it for now). There were a couple of L=A=N=G=U=A=G=E poets. There was at least one formalist and one feminist, and a handful who would become, after Stephen Burt coined the term, Elliptical poets. And each of these schools, these styles, these whatever-you-want-to-call-them, had their own manifesto, a set of written or unwritten laws governing what was and was not "good poetry."

As a writer, I've always thought that labeling things, putting them into discreet and identifiable boxes, was more the work of academics than of artists. Most artists I know are more interested in making art than they are in writing critical, analytical papers or dissertations or books about the how and when and why of various styles or schools of it. As writers, some of us, particularly those of us who teach, do like to talk about the craft of writing, but that's something else completely. Simply put, artists make art. It's someone else's job to label it, file it, and intellectualize it. Now, I'm not some kind of anti-intellectual. I love reading and sometimes even writing that stuff (maybe that's what I'm doing right now!) But I do believe that, if you're a poet, writing poetry should come first. If, on the other hand, you spend more time obsessing about the style of poetry you write, or trying to figure out to which school of poetry you belong, perhaps you're not a poet at all. Perhaps you're Helen Vendler.

For me, all of this circles back around to our current age of polarization. I've witnessed writers attacking one another (on paper or in speeches, of course) for belonging to the wrong school of poetics, for writing the wrong kind of poetry. I've experienced such attacks myself. And I have to ask, quite plainly, what is the point? Is our need to be right, to be on top, in control, so innate that we can't, with intelligence and empathy and creativity, overcome it? We're writers, after all. Aren't we supposed to be creating the work that calls attention to and critiques the flaws in our own society, and sometimes even offers healthier alternatives? It's fine if you want to be in your own particular school of poetics.

I'm happy to range around through all of them, looking for anything that will challenge me, make me a better writer. If any of us still feel the need to live in opposition to something or someone, remember, there are a lot of people out there who would prefer that we not write at all, no matter what poetic traditions we embrace. There are people out there who would do away with freedom of the press, close down most publishers, and leave us all sitting in a creative and critical void. I know that's not us, not the artists and writers of the world, that's them, whoever they may be, and in order to work against them, to thwart their desire to silence the dialogue that literature and art creates, we have to do what we do first and best: write. Just write.

David Mura

MY SON AT NINTH GRADE

Overnight grown so towering, head wooly
with long curls, he'll stare me down eye
to eye. A black wisp over his lip he

won't shave. Hip-hop on I-pod, beats
on Garage Band, poems on his Mac
book. And nights beneath the sheets

whispering on his cell to Yasmine,
a twenty-first century down low romance
her father and brothers would shut down

like a house of plague...if they discovered.
I pass his door and his voice lowers.
What does she see in him and he in her?

Only it's not sight, there in the dark,
but the words shuttling between them,
old as Romeo and Juliet, Sharks

and Jets, Buddha and Mohammed
and the mad crazy years we live in
where this young love fights to flourish.

(Two weeks later her brother shouts
the alarm to her father and mother. Now
there's a line that cannot be crossed,

and still I hear my son behind his door
weeping and whispering in the dark,
voices on the line, their secrets abhorred.)

*

Once a white boy fell in love with my aunt.
She left for the camps, never saw him again.
Ojii-san disapproved. He was from Japan.

Five young Somali men shot or knifed
last year in our precinct. Others vanished
to Mogadishu, war lords, civil strife.

The FBI, the police, what do they know?
Fathers, mothers, where's your daughter, your son?
Children, all this started so long ago.

Tonight as I make our bed, my son sneaks
in, leaps my back with his heavy new body;
and with war yelps wrestles me to the sheets.

Of course I don't let him beat me. Grunting
back, I toss him off like the years, grapple
his torso down, pinion each young wing,

though even as he cries out *I give, I give*,
assenting to the father, I cannot grip
him tight enough, I cannot let go.

Bryce Parsons-Twesten

Bryce Parsons-Twesten of the Knox Writers' House answers some questions

The brainchild of three Knox College English majors, Knox Writer's House is a virtual house found online at knoxwritershouse.com. It's a Winchester-Mansion-like, always-being-built abode lavish with "poems, stories, essays, and interviews of nearly one hundred writers from Chicago to Madison to the Twin Cities to Kalamazoo to St. Louis to Kansas City . . . going south to New Orleans, east to Atlanta, further east to New York, New Haven, Providence." When you go to the KWH homepage, you find a Google map of the United States—literally, a "map of voices"—with interactive green Google teardrops marking the places where each of the recorded writers live, a click being the only distance between you and a wealth of voices, a wealth of words. This interview is with one of the founders.

Matt Mauch: *If you had to capture the essence of your venture in a promotional short form like a book blurb—you know, three to five lightning-rod sentences—what would you say (and hint: keep these for your press releases)?*

Bryce Parsons-Twesten: This week on Astounding Stories, three young travelers search the country for the voice of America! Poetry! Stories! The entire Addie chapter of *As I Lay Dying*! Hear the voices of writers you love! Hear the voices of writers you will love! Just press play!

MM: *Back in the print era, I and some business partners (which may or may not be hard to come to terms with, but is what you all are) started up a Village Voice-esque publication in a medium-sized Midwestern city. One of the greatest parts of the start-up was researching all that was out there—driving from city to city to collect each city's weekly so we didn't reinvent the wheel (unless doing so was appropriate). What, for you, has been greatest part of The Knox Writers' House start-up?*

BPT: It sounds like you put a lot more forethought into your undertaking than we put into ours. Emily had the idea to start recording people reading their poems and poems they loved by other writers, then we decided to expand it together and we jumped in feet first. It's difficult to pick a greatest part of that. Waking up on a stranger's floor, forcing ourselves awake and out to the car, following the GPS to the next house, praying they will offer us coffee, getting to know a stranger, hearing beautiful poems sitting in a new kitchen 2,000 miles from home. Every trip was a wonderful collection of trials and tribulations and honest connections with strangers.

MM: *What's in the basement of The Knox Writers' House? What, that is, are the things, people, experiences, etc., that inspired you to build it, and remain, albeit underground, as your foundation?*

BPT: Aside from the skeletons and Christmas presents we're hoping to re-gift next year, the Poetry Foundation is a major piece of the, er, foundation. I used to spend hours on their website listening to poems, and it's a totally different way to encounter things you've never read before. Having the pace at which you ingest a poem or a story decided for you changes everything—it returns it to the form of a spell, of something that's put down one piece at a time, that establishes one thing, then adds to it and adds to it and adds to it until it, and hopefully whoever is listening, is something else entirely. Looking over a poem in a book, you can ruin that for yourself. Of course there's also nothing else like sitting silently with a book and being changed, but they're different kinds of magic. Sam and Emily and I all took a class at Knox on Ulysses and when we were assigned the first chapter, I read it aloud to Emily, and I felt physically changed after I read it. It really is like a spell. Going to readings at Knox also informed how I thought about The Knox Writers' House. It was always startling to go to a student reading and hear someone you didn't even know was a writer, who you'd seen around campus and smoking outside at parties, read something incredible. I was continually finding out about the amazing art people around me were making when they went home at night. It didn't seem fair that I didn't know these things all along. All this, and Emily and Sam and I have spent a lot of time reading aloud to each other.

MM: *You came over to my house after a night at Pocket Lab, followed by cocktails at the 331, on a sultry-ass summer day when we may have actually broken a dew-point record in these Cities Twin, recording me and another TC poet and in the process christening my version of that Minnesota staple, the basement bar. I only have the one story, but you've got to have hundreds. What have been some of the cooler or crazier things you've done that you'll one day wax nostalgic about?*

BPT: Oh, there are so many to choose from. When we first came to the Twin Cities to record writers, we were still new to what we were doing, and we weren't sure exactly how it would go or how people would respond, and one of our first nights there, we went to meet Paula Cisewski at her house. Her husband Jack was there, and Sarah Fox and John Colburn, and we all started on this uncharted, exciting, uncomfortable, fantastic journey together, talking about art and poetry and what it meant to be a writer and an artist and how you participate in a community and if you need that, or if you want that, and how, exactly, do you live your life as a person and live your life as an artist, and how do you find the time for your passion, and how cold, exactly, does Minneapolis get, and what does it mean that sometimes only poets go to poetry readings and does it matter, and does any of this matter, and what, really, truly, is the Midwest? We were in way over our heads and being swept along in ways we couldn't have hoped to be swept along. After we left, we sat in the car and took out the poem "first impression," printed on a piece of paper John had brought with him and read from and given to us, and we sat in the dark car and read it aloud again, and maybe I'm imagining it, but in my mind, we looked at each other, a little raw and wide-eyed, amazed at what we had found. There was also the time I got strep in Chicago and my face swelled up to twice its size and Sam read me to sleep with *Jesus' Son* by Denis Johnson. That was a great time.

MM: *So, softball question time. There are poetry sites out there, like the $100 million Poetry Foundation site. Poets, publishers, and the poetically inclined have 'em linked and bookmarked. As the new kid on the block, what doth distinguish The Knox Writers' House (I call this a softball question because I think there are oodles of things that make you you)?*

BPT: When I described what we were doing to a great friend of mine, and showed him the draft of the website I was working on, he described it as an everyman's *Paris Review*. Of course we don't come anywhere near the greatness of that publication, but I like that. It's exciting to me that we've put on record some voices that are not widely heard. Voices that have written great poems and stories, but that aren't known outside of their communities. There are writers on our website that are well known—there are writers on our website that have been in *The Paris Review*—but there are also great writers I had never heard of and am thrilled to have found. John Colburn is a great example. "first impression" affected me. I can still recite lines from it. And it is a great resource to make that available to people, to have that out there. And though our method was sporadic, and the way we found writers was far from methodical, it is a view of what is happening right now in writing in the United States. It's like when we were students at Knox and we discovered that someone we had known in passing for years had been working hard writing poetry that whole time. You can go to knoxwritershouse.com and find a little list of people who live in your city, who live down the street from you, who are working hard to make art. And that little list should remind you that really, every other person you meet is devoting themselves to poetry of some kind or another.

MM: *If the GOD OF THINGS HENCE came to you in the form of a boxelder bug and asked, job-interview style, "Where do you see yourself five years from now?" what would say about The Knox Writers' House? Will you still be recording poets? Will you have expanded? Will you become a nonprofit? Will you expand services? How will the world have changed because of you? Tell us what you see in your crystal ball.*

BPT: I'd tell that little bug, who knows. We all live in different zip codes now, so it changes things a bit. In five years, we could each be recording writers in the places we live, then every once in a while, taking a bus to Argentina and stopping in every city along the way. Maybe in five years there will actually be a house for The Knox Writers' House. Who knows, little bug, who knows.

MM: *What about The Knox Writers' House lifeblood, i.e., you as an individual person—what are you up to? Striving for? Thinking about? Making? Selling? Studying? Writing? Doing? Give us a glimpse into the reality show you call your life.*

BPT: Right now I'm trying to live well, enjoy life, and still make something of myself while looking for a job with student loans sitting on my shoulders. I'm working on a million things at once. I'm always starting new ideas. I just hope to finish two percent of what I start.

MM: *And you're moving to the Twin Cities when?*

BPT: As soon as you get the fold out bed ready. I'll bring my pillow.

Heid E. Erdrich

PAINT THESE STREETS

for Frank Big Bear

Paint these streets, paint them over.

Paint grass acid green over gray asphalt,
hot orange rivers over white chalk marks,
indigo clouds over yellow police tape.

Paint these streets.
Paint them bright.
Where those dive-bars once bled out tumbling figures,
in senseless colors, and dull shades of death in the alley,
under the bridge, beside the highway—paint it over.
Paint it *all over.*

Paint it so it lights up—sends fear howling off and away,
like the monster dog it is, yelping at fire, heart's passion,
action.

Paint these streets.
Paint them alive.

Where ones we loved once stumbled, dying senselessly,
drained to blank canvasses—those very stoops, curbs, rails:
Paint them full, vibrating with strokes of purple, pink, cerise.

Paint their faces.
Paint them lit from within, composed of fantastic leaves,
shards of jewels,
cut-glass beads,
and the radiance of survival in a community thriving.

Paint these streets, paint them over.
Tell another story,

one that does not forget what formed the muddy storm
in the background, the contrast to today's lightning strikes—
organized bolts of energy, all our work,
what it takes to transform.

Paint these streets.
Paint them over with vivid possibilities.
Neon green, brilliant blue—day-glo lives striding home,
where we *are* home,
in the strobe
that lights up ordinary lives
in work, in art, in motion.

Sharon Chmielarz

Finding a Soul-Scape

Emotional typography: You know its terrain, mountains, peaks, valleys, plains. But I'm thinking here of soul-scape, what Beckett called the physical landscape that matches a writer's soul. Since it fills the vacancy in the heart, it is as significant and lucky to find as a soul-mate. I think of it not only in terms of room/space, but also as time-as-place. Love, longing, and restlessness drive us in search for its "forever."

I'd say this quest comes from the long ago when humankind was cast from the womb's ocean. "Out of the cradle endlessly rocking..." Or, more recently in the human chain of events, out of a Ford's back seat. After the ocean, we inhabited a mythical place for a few months. You can call it the Garden of Eden, the place where everything was perfect. A kind of Schlaraffenland, where you only had to think of what you wanted–buffalo wings!–and open your mouth. It flew in. You felt complete, at home, the welcoming idyll baseball replays during each game. Home and its landscape.

As a teenager I hated the landscape I was born in. It felt to me, with all its South Dakota big sky barrenness, claustrophobic. I was lost in a tiny, four-walled house. I'd have argued that my surroundings bore no resemblance whatsoever to my soul (had I thought in those terms). I was an orphan left by some brutal twist of fate on the Northern Plain's rugged, intense sparseness. I longed to regain my real home, a two-story brick house in Connecticut with professors for parents. What was I doing here? With a mother cowed by my father, my father in sweaty glasses and blue coveralls.

My Baptist prayer mantra then was, "I look up to the hills, from whence cometh my help." And that help was to endure, to find the way out. But can your soul-scape be something you pray to escape? Or, is loathing an early stage in finding the soul-scape? What about the years your early landscape impressed itself upon you, claimed you, without you noticing?

From our front door, over the railroad tracks, the view opened to fields in the Missouri River Valley and the river itself. Its chain of hills, a feature on the horizon which in South Dakota is a shoreline impossible to reach. You can try. You will fail. Despite its similarity to a sea scape (and indeed once it was a huge sea floor), a boat on this scape is useless. But in my childhood you could take a train. And since the depot was only a few blocks walk from our house, it was a position not unlike an Irishman who goes down to the wharf to sail away from his village.

"And murmuring under, pervading all, I'd bring the rustling sea-sound,/ That endless sound from the two Great Seas of the world. *" ("Thou Mother with They Equal Brood," #2, Walt Whitman.)*

As a sixth grader in geography class I dreamed of the places I'd like to visit as traveler–Russia, Argentina, the Andes. (I loved the name "Andes." More intimate than "Rockies.") Curious that none of these places were in the States. Their very foreignness appealed to me. They were far enough away that I could play the role of towered victim yearning after a love she could not reach.

When you believe your soul-scape lies in an unknown landscape, perhaps you have visited it or lived there vicariously through books, photos, stories, dreams, and it is waiting your discovery/ or physical presence?

I'm as pragmatic as the next, but the idea of time as soul-place I find delightful. Theo Dorgan, the Irish poet, calls it time-collapse. It's a deja vu-like feeling but lasting longer. It makes another (distant) place and time present within an "our time" place: the past with us and extending backward and toward at once. You are caught in the present which is happening 5000 years ago.

An example: One night in the former Cafe Amore on Milton & Grand in St. Paul I saw a man who resembled exactly in dress and facial features and hair Van Gogh in his Self Portrait. He sat at a table talking tete a tete to a young woman. I tried not to stare, but my god! A rush of impressions overwhelmed me–from van Gogh's paintings, from his letters to his brother, from having had lunch in a little cafe in Kraków called "Van Gogh's" –a rush of different places and different times. Though I was in St Paul, I was not. For a moment, something–X in my soul-scape?–met with the hour. In this collapsed time, I felt the lovely recognition of being totally alive NOW and THEN, the Then as Now-Continued.

I'm too rational to believe in re-incarnation, but who is the I we are when we fall into these time warps, in this case, St. Paul and van Gogh's time in Arles collapsed? Or maybe the time was Milton and Grand and a cafe in the Bournasage where van Gogh painted potato fields? Or maybe, all concurrently. This is kin to but not quite like time machine travel during a movie or an engaging novel. We connect with a certain soul scape, its time and place.

There's another phenomenon to be considered as soul-scape, and it happens when the past is incorporated as place and time through voice, i.e., when the poet/ writer seems inhabited by another voice or time. The voice's point of view may differ from the actual landscape bequeathed the writer at birth, but it must in some way attract, lure the writer, and arrive in the present on the writer's love for or profound interest in a particular period or place, whether s/he's lived there or not.

I remember while working on the manuscript which later became *The Other Mozart* how shocked I'd be after spending the morning in my mind at the Mozart flat in Salzburg to find myself in Cub grocery shopping. What was this place? Who were these people?

Someone once asked the ballet dancer, Baryshnikov, if he were ever homesick for Russia. He replied he had no homeland, neither in Russia or here. His only home was the stage where ever in the world it might be. Some writers might say the same of the blank space on the page. This is the space, albeit white and barren, where the imagination can come out from behind the curtains and find a stage on which to thrive.

There's a paradox in this. To convey their imaginative scapes, writers must work with the rational: Words. Wallace Stevens refers to "flawed words and stubborn sounds." Of all people, writers have a sensory attachment to language. They are at home among words. They have an interest in, an affair with words. They find a welcoming place/page among words, words are features on the soul-scape of the page. Making a line or paragraph is like tending a house we love. "No other words but words of love," Walt Whitman writes, "no other thought but love." (from "From Noon to Starry Night" section 5) .

Not long ago I heard Charles Baxter say on MPR, " Your imagination's home has to look like something." I agree, but if you were to ask I couldn't tell you exactly what this looks like, where my soul scape is. I should amend that: Maybe I haven't yet accepted my soul-scape. Maybe it looks like the place I have such mixed feelings about, that dreaded prairie! And yet, its pull: After so many years of living away from it, the hunger I have some days to leave the city and drive out under its huge, beautiful, fierce, claustrophobic sky.

There's no guarantee when you find your soulscape or if you'll find it. If you live apart, not a part of, you have the advantage of being able to be present in two places at once. Your real world with its traffic lights and asphalt and Cub stores, and the one you seek. "One place understood," Eudora Welty said, "helps us understand all places better." I understand the woods, the sea, the mountains, because of the prairie's scape which I can't escape, my own soul-scape?

Do you know yours? "Maybe," Emily Dickinson suggests, "it would puzzle us, To find our way home..."

DOORS

We sang the way drunks across America do, arms slung across
shoulders, faces red with the failed effort of forcing words
to stand straight and form lines of coherent sentences,
hands holding beers to the air to counterbalance

our new-found stupidity. This was years ago, in the doorway
of the Boston Cafe, two of us facing those we'd lost at the bar
hours earlier. We put on a show, yelling, "Hello, I love you
won't you tell me your name," until a cook, greasy as the food
he made, threw a spatula, and threatened to call the cops.

I hadn't see Tommy in years. He'd thinned out into a man
and maybe I'd done the same, but there we stood, acting like boys, drunk on
goodwill and each others' company. Months later
I drew the shade on that part of my life and stumbled toward

sobriety. Mornings are kind to me now. I pour cereal and set
out coats and hats and gloves and boots. I kiss my boys off to school
and my wife back to sleep. At night I'm tired and wouldn't see last call
if bars closed at eleven. I haven't seen Tommy since

and most likely never will. Our lives have followed the small-town trajectory
of leaving and return trips that gradually trail off into a day that never comes.
But each time The Doors shake the carnival loose from a radio

I see Tommy and me framed in the doorway of cockiness and brotherhood.
In my heart those days are gone, thought the silhouette of my old life
reaches toward my new self and throws an arm over my shoulder
and says that Tommy is waiting, and that I never meant to be gone for good.

Cullen Bailey Burns

A review of Lisa Fishman's *Flower Cart* (Ahsahta Press)

Lisa Fishman's beautiful, challenging *Flower Cart* is
unlike any book of poems I have read. Her poems intersect
with and surround a trio of found texts, each of which
poses questions about authorship and reading. Ultimately,
Fishman's experimental and expansive poems explore the
generative "materia" of domestic life and enact the difficulty
of articulating "what is most real" upon the page.

Flower Cart begins with found text, a letter reproduced
on the book's first page. Written by the Superintendent of
the Milwaukee County School of Agriculture and Domestic
Economy, dated March 16, 1916, the letter is apparently
responding to an inquiry regarding the quality of a sample
of corn. The writer advises the inquirer against using the
seed because it "includes a distinct mixture of at least three
different varieties of corn." This letter is a puzzling and
intriguing start to a book of poems. Eventually it becomes
clear that, in addition to situating the book in its rural
Wisconsin landscape, the letter cautions Fishman's readers:
like the seed, this book is cross-pollinated; it "does not
possess the characteristics of any one particular variety."

Fishman's poems surround this and the other found texts
and begin to highlight the ways she is using these materials
to explore questions of authorship and meaning. The book's
first poem, "As it would seem, to have netted" is characteristic
of the book's style. It has a title that acts as a first line; lines
without punctuation; a "you" who sometimes seems to be
the reader and other times an intimate of the speaker. The
book's central ideas are also found in this poem: "I meant to
ask/did you find a place/to accompany me, materia / in the
hybrid form/and so became...." We find here a sense of space
between intent and action ("I meant to ask"). Further, the
speaker indicates that her material is "hybrid," a mixture.
Finally, the words "and so became" suggest that meaning

is not fixed but is a process of becoming (also indicated by the poem ending with no closing mark of punctuation), an argument made by most of the poems in the book.

The second found text in *Flower Cart* is from an old notebook. A facsimile of the notebook's cover appears in the book. "Herald Square: A notebook for speed and efficiency...the leaves turn swiftly and lie flat...the book will stand alone for transcribing...." Fishman explains in her acknowledgments that this section of the book is made up of contents "transcribed" from the notebook. Apparently, she has taken the cover at its word. But in her transcriptions, Fishman seems to reshape (we can't be certain as the original text does not appear) the original in a variety of ways. We find lists of numbers:

April 3 Monday
40 employees
7-14-1965
1000s of eggs

and lists of questions:

Why didn't you answer my letter?
To whom are you speaking?
Why don't you sew in the morning?

and lists of words arranged by vowel sounds:

moonlight
loophole
juke box
hoof print

These lists are notable for the ways in which words are arranged sonically, as well as for their compound nature. "Moonlight" and "loophole" are compound words, but "juke box" and "hoof print" are a form of compounding too. There are many such words here (waffle iron, lumber yard, sauce pan, pawn shop, to name just a few). In these meetings, joining noun to noun, another object emerges, in the way that a waffle and an iron are different things than a waffle iron. Even the book's title, *Flower Cart*, creates of flowers and a cart an image of beauty and movement, overflowing with blossom and possibility. Similarly, Fishman suggests, the meeting of found text with her own presents opportunity for a new entity greater than the sum of its parts.

This "Herald Square" section of the book demonstrates the intersections of past and present, word and word, author and author and reader. But when the book returns to Fishman's own writing, I am struck by the unavoidable comparison in diction and imagery and can't help but notice how much more beautiful her own words are.

That the poem following the "Herald Square" section is called "Reading" highlights Fishman's desire to explore the questions raised by her reading/rewriting of the notebook text. It begins: "A number of transitional objects/starting with one/ may be meant." Meant by the author? Or do the objects contain their meaning intrinsically? The next line offers even more possibilities. "There are certain things I don't mean." What are these things? Words that have been written? Spoken? Qualities of the speaker herself? And the next line "what a pleasure to say" suggests further complication. Is the pleasure in saying things she doesn't mean? Or is it a pleasure to speak in general? To find the space between utterance and meaning?

Notably, here, as throughout the book, a sense of play informs the poem. The speaker's pleasure in language and possibility asks us to make meaning for ourselves, to enjoy letting "your intelligence run away with you." Fishman takes the play seriously—this is a carefully crafted work—and the poem's last lines remind us to read closely, for "there is so much that happens/ in the little words."

Reading attentively is especially important in the long poem "KabbaLoom" in which *Flower Cart's* themes and explorations come together. The movement of text across the page becomes even more important in this poem, as does use of white space, with some pages containing just one line of text.

The poem begins with several columns of words. The relationship between some of the words is clear ("matrix" and "womb," "linen" and "line") but other times elusive ("cloth" and "hotel"). Even without understanding how all the columns of words are related, we can see that the words suggest something about creating and the material needed for that creation: a loom, a body, a needle and cloth. The creative act working across the page can be see in this line:

"shine: s/he, i

              n   new"

The anagram of "shine" in the intimate relation of "s/he, i" becomes something new, possible, from language and body.
    Later in the poem, we see this idea explored more fully:

"if letters can house a word
then words are not made of letters but letters are made of words
a shape makes a letter   a body"

The images of sewing, of the loom, recur. The word play continues to emphasize double meanings—textile becomes "text Isle" and fabricate becomes "fabric I ate" "because I do not sew." The weaving of linen becomes "linen? line n" and we can see the page created from the linen, upon which the words lie, and the line the words create. The speaker tells us she is "—just trying to see the shapes, to see inside". Her exploration necessitates our own; for us to understand what's inside, we must accompany her opening up of space and language to see what's there.
    Language can be a form of intimacy, too. In a later selection of the poem, the speaker says:

we have the hotel and the loam

       o, tell   o, am

Here, "hotel" "o, tell" and "loam" "o, am," link language to being, suggesting that the story (o, tell) creates the existence (o, am). The hotel and loam, furthermore, evoke meeting places for lovers and the generative soil, both potent places of intersection. This poem ends with an image of the body shining, "ribbed" and closes with the word "bode". In addition to suggesting the bowed ribcage, the last word is a beginning, both a command and a premonition. The end—again with no closing mark of punctuation—refuses conclusion.

In this remarkable book, Lisa Fishman asks us to read and reread texts, to explore the results of her restless pressing together of ideas and time and material. At the intersection of found and new text, meaning is less important, ultimately, than possibility: "midsummer dream//of the etymon, a comedy". Modification and corruption of the original are not only inevitable, they are necessary. And enjoyable. In the last line of the book, the speaker ponders graffiti on the moon as she travels across the county, and she comes to the conclusion that "I might be able to think about that." This line seems to me a perfect ending—open and conditional— for an ambitious book that challenges our expectations and desire to know. Certainly I will think about *Flower Cart*, a beautiful and stunning book, for a long time.

Kyle Adamson

DEBRIEFING

"Is that a WMD in your pocket,
or are you just happy to see me?"
I asked Syed.

I fumbled through his bent-over keister
like an electrician in a dark fuse box.

But I found nothing but a Yale diploma &
one jumbo sized *Mission Accomplished* banner.

Elbow deep, I plunged,
"None in here, but this Hajji sure has
one clean colon," I muttered.

I almost felt bad for the rubber glove
that I wasn't wearing.

Deeper, I reached; & I discovered
that I went too far. I plowed past the point
where one could find Osama Bin Laden or
the logic behind the Homeland Security Act.

I reached even farther &
rescued a CNN reporter before
she was beheaded by masked terrorists,

But it wasn't until I was shoulder deep
that I found the *shock & awe*.

I even found the Holy Grail,
but I wasn't looking for that.

"No WMD's in here, Sergeant!" I said
punting the Grail into the Euphrates River.

Joyce Sutphen

Poems into Poems

I began memorizing poems when I was old, but younger than I am now. At first it was an attempt to fill time when I was working at a job that didn't require much thinking or talking, so I memorized "The Tyger," by William Blake, a poem that I had always loved for its rhythm and images. The next thing I memorized was Shakespeare's "Sonnet 60"— I can't remember what prompted that choice, but I was fond of the way the sound of the first line, "Like as the waves make towards the pebbled shore," seemed to replicate (in a funny way) the sound of waves coming in on the shore.

Not long after the boring job, I decided to go to graduate school, where I took courses in literary studies, creative writing (emphasis in fiction and memoir), and began work on a dissertation in Shakespeare studies. My topic turned out to be memory—Shakespeare and just about anything that had to do with remembering and forgetting. I started out interested in the political aspects of memory in *Hamlet*, but I soon became intrigued with the lost "arte of memorie," which seemed to have been buried by the printed page and the sands of time. Along the way I learned how important it once had been to have texts archived in the mind, so that a person had their own private library always available—and, to make a long story very short, I decided that I would try to memorize as many poems as I could.

Since a major portion of my dissertation had to do with the way memory worked in Shakespeare's *Sonnets*, I thought it might be a good idea to memorize as many of those as I could—especially ones that had to do with my topic, figuring that if I knew a poem inside and out, I might have something interesting to say about it. I also thought I might come to understand memory (and the process of memorizing) better if I was more actively involved—though it was disappointing to discover that I myself did not *naturally* have a good memory; I really had to work at getting a poem imprinted in the "book and volume" of my brain!

I had plenty of time for learning and relearning lines each morning and evening as I commuted to work at a small college about an hour away from my home. I was ABD when I took the job—and it probably postponed the completion of my dissertation by a year or so, but two things about it were especially important to me as a poet: the first was that from the start people at this college encouraged me as a poet (even though I had only published a few poems), and the second was that the commute gave me a perfect amount of time and space to memorize and think about poems. I had begun writing poems a year or so earlier—partly because I wanted a break from the big prose project of the dissertation, and partly because learning those sonnets in the car had started me thinking in terms of the little room that a poem makes— especially one as structured as the sonnet. I began to think of ways to fill that room.

My first poems weren't formal, nor were they in form, but they were influenced (I can see that now) by the themes of the things I was archiving in my head: for instance, when I began a poem with the phrase "That is not the country" and ended the line with "for poetry," I was thinking (although unconsciously) about Yeats's poem "Sailing to Byzantium," which begins with "That is not the country for old men," and about the landscape of farms and small towns that I was seeing along my drive. When I thought about Death, "checking me out," it was, I realize now, a continuation of Emily Dickinson's personification of Death, carried into my body. There are all sorts of places in my first and second books where I see the influence of what I was memorizing and thinking about, sometimes to an almost excessive degree. Take this poem from my second book (*Coming Back to the Body*):

Her Legendary Head

This is the way the woman in
a Picasso painting feels, with her
mobile nose holding two eyes

to one side, her quivering lip
ascending into a pointed chin.

The world is now (and she
can hear its roar) all a blood-
dimmed tide, things fall
apart and then together, banged
and whimpering they begin.

All her life, she was up to
her neck in marble, and
the gyres in her head. Just
another woman in pieces,
inventory lost, instructions

too small to read. Broken
the lines of her, a memorially
reconstructed version, awaiting
the detection of each separate
and mysterious error.

    The title, for starters, comes from Rilke. I had
recently memorized that lovely poem, "The Archaic Torso of
Apollo," which begins with "We cannot know his legendary
head," and I'd fallen in love with the combination of
"legendary" and "head." Who knows why—I just loved it,
but actually, the title came last. What came first was the
absolutely genuine statement: "This is the way the woman in
/ a Picasso painting feels," followed by an attempt to evoke
the distorted face of a Picasso woman.
    The next stanza has traces of "Dover Beach" ("she
/ can hear its 'roar'") and "The Second Coming" ("things fall
apart") and "The Hollow Men" ("banged / and whimpering").
It's a very unfriendly world—a "Wasteland."
    The third stanza is partly Picasso again, thinking
of the cubist (and often massive) shapes used to present
women, partly Yeats ("gyres") and partly pun ("gyres" evoking
"gears"), ending with another genuine statement: "Just /
another woman in pieces / inventory lost, instructions / to

small to read."

The last stanza isn't so much an echo of memorized lines, but a reflection on the faultiness of memory—and the unsteady sense that despite a skillful glue job, this woman has been broken and someone—a very careful observer, a reader of poems perhaps—will be able to see that.

As time goes by, I continue to memorize poems—my composition practices always lagging slightly behind what I've stored in my memory (and bones, I like to think). It took years for me to write a (fairly) perfect Shakespearean sonnet, though I experimented voluminously with a whole array of ways to arrange fourteen lines of (most often) ten syllables. I began to have an uncanny sense of iambic pentameter and a premonition when I had reached the penultimate line. Meanwhile, I am memorizing longer things—Wallace Steven's "Sunday Morning" and Elizabeth Bishop's "Invitation to Miss Marianne Moore"; I haven't written anything like either of these, but I think about them often—as I do poems by Emily Dickinson and Theodore Roethke that live in my memory. They make good company, if nothing else.

Anh-Hoa Thi Nguyen

ONE SIX FIVE

You cried when I left for California – you and Ba standing in the driveway, never separate. I didn't expect that from you – wasn't prepared for the weeping that would last until I crossed the state border.

When I got to Oakland, my emotions unleashed like a wildfire, and I had no way of putting them out, and they were the kind that combust and destroy you – your security, your shell.

It almost killed me – the homesickness, the longing, the guilt and anger that swelled itself into a stone in my throat. 165 days till I see you again. How many days in a semester? How long before I can go home?

Sometimes you need to burn everything to begin anew. And here there are no seasons – the deaths are not as severe, the purification not as complete. For years now, I've been holding on to my desire for incineration – to let the nature of the sun have its way with me – to feel the green tips of grass force their way through the ashes of earth – the complicated earth that seems so soft at the surface, and yet so deep.

That is how I feel – the hidden layers of hardness, then liquid, then flame. Can anything survive at the core, endure the intensity? Must I always hold people at a distance – never let them settle inside me?

Mother, there is not enough room for me in your womb anymore. That is why I left – to seek a new home for myself, a place where I could grow again.

165 miles that I cried
165 times I missed you today
165 meals that did not satisfy
165 was not the number of my dorm room, or my first apartment, or my last
165 dollars for a one-way ticket
(651) the area code home

Sam Conrad

Sam Conrad of the Knox Writers' House answers some questions

The brainchild of three Knox College English majors, Knox Writer's House is a virtual house found online at knoxwritershouse.com. It's a Winchester-Mansion-like, always-being-built abode lavish with "poems, stories, essays, and interviews of nearly one hundred writers from Chicago to Madison to the Twin Cities to Kalamazoo to St. Louis to Kansas City . . . going south to New Orleans, east to Atlanta, further east to New York, New Haven, Providence." When you go to the KWH homepage, you find a Google map of the United States—literally, a "map of voices"—with interactive green Google teardrops marking the places where each of the recorded writers live, a click being the only distance between you and a wealth of voices, a wealth of words. This interview is with one of the founders.

Matt Mauch: *If you had to capture the essence of your venture in a promotional short form like a book blurb—you know, three to five lightning-rod sentences—what would you say (and hint: keep these for your press releases)?*

Sam Conrad: Where does writing continue to live and breathe today? The Knox Writers' House ventured forth and crawled deep into the skin-folds of the American landscape to find the answer and to bring focus to the contemporary sources of writing life. In rustic kitchens, book-soaked offices and every imaginable space in-between, words and friendships danced until they settled into the woodwork of the Knox Writers' House—an audio archival website, but also, a heartfelt conversation between regions, readers and writers.

MM: *Back in the print era, I and some business partners (which may or may not be hard to come to terms with, but is what you all are) started up a Village Voice-esque publication in a medium-*

sized Midwestern city. One of the greatest parts of the start-up was researching all that was out there—driving from city to city to collect each city's weekly so we didn't reinvent the wheel (unless doing so was appropriate). What, for you, has been greatest part of The Knox Writers' House start-up?

SC: Honestly, the best (and worst?) part of the start-up was not knowing where to start, a problem/benefit I'm sure you ran into with your own publication. I was brought into the project after Emily had already fleshed out a skeleton for where the project was heading, but it was exciting getting in a rented car and driving to our first destination (Madison?) not really knowing what the hell to expect. We didn't have plans to interview people, we didn't have plans to do a best-loved; we had plans to enjoy each others' company, dig collectively into this passion of ours (people and literature), and see what we lucked into. Emily's enthusiasm, in short, was the best part of the start-up. With that infectious smile on our side, details didn't matter. We flew by the seat of our pants and it changed our lives.

MM: *What's in the basement of The Knox Writers' House? What, that is, are the things, people, experiences, etc., that inspired you to build it, and remain, albeit underground, as your foundation?*

SC: Dozens of empty jars of peanut butter, jugs of orange juice, boxes of corn-syrup packed snacks. I would say those things were our foundation and basement during the actual building of the House. Hahaha. But really, my inspiration started with Emily. She believed so much in whatever this project was going to become that I had confidence in our construction skills even without any carpentry knowledge to build on. Okay, enough with that conceit. Our mentor and projectmom Monica believed in us, our former professor and now-friend Beth believed in us, and everybody that we spoke to, these amazing and well-respected writers talking to these three ragtag hippy wordfreaks, seemed to believe in us, and just a few kind words from these people (you) fortified our belief in the project. In our first city, Madison, we had no clue what the hell we were doing. Straight up, no lie, no idea. We had a microphone, a pretty dysfunctional Macbook, and smiles. That's it. We wouldn't have kept going, maybe just me, if the first few people we talked to were like, "Oh, you're just a bunch of kids. Do you know what the hell you're doing? Why should I trust you with my life's breath?" You're all, all your writers and friends, are in our basement doing kegstands, is what I'm trying to say.

MM: *You came over to my house after a night at Pocket Lab, followed by cocktails at the 331, on a sultry-ass summer day when we may have actually broken a dew-point record in these Cities Twin, recording me and another TC poet and in the process christening my version of that Minnesota staple, the basement bar. I only have the one story, but you've got to have hundreds. What have been some of the cooler or crazier things you've done that you'll one day wax nostalgic about?*

SC: I think that the sampler pack Matt (Ryan) hooked us all up with let us keep the humidity out of our minds (I mean, your guys' writing was pretty aight, too). Man, what won't we wax nostalgic about one day? Paula and Jack's house where we chilled with them and Sarah and John in the Twin Cities was really the first moment we were like, "Whoa, this is (fuckin) awesome." We were just four kids sitting in these amazing writers' kitchen and we shot the shit about life, writing—everything. When we got back to the car, we sat there unmoving for several minutes just in disbelief with the amazing time we just had. There's all the people we couch surfed with that ended up being some of the most interesting and coolest people we met on our journeys and opened their floors and couches and fridges to us. There's visigoth-ing a quite nice potluck some kids from Macalester College threw like only Knox College kids know who to do. There's almost getting kicked out of Prairie Lights bookstore in Iowa City because we were having too much fun with Jericho Brown and Amber Dermont. There's super gluing our car back together in Chicago. There's Bryce catching the plague in Chicago and champing his way through every appointment we had. To name a few.

MM: *So, softball question time. There are poetry sites out there, like the $100 million Poetry Foundation site. Poets, publishers, and the poetically inclined have 'em linked and bookmarked. As the new kid on the block, what doth distinguish The Knox Writers' House (I call this a softball question because I think there are oodles of things that make you you)?*

SC: THE $100 MILLION POETRY FOUNDATION WEBSITE. Man, we met in Iowa City the dude that helped put that together (Nick Twemlow) and were like, "man you musta spent $20,000 on that website," and he just laughed at us. I think the fact that we didn't have a million dollars to do this is crucial. Before this past summer, only Emily got paid and, frankly, it wasn't much and most of it went towards food cost and extra gas and life expenses (thanks Emily, and Monica, you're the best).

We went to these writers' kitchen tables—invaded their lives, soothed their babies, ate their food, took off our shoes. I don't think many sites or projects out there are doing that. It's the difference between the "you come to us and be happy that we're letting you be a part of our website/ project/whatever" and "what...you mean, you'll talk to us, Ralph Angel? Like, you're willing to take an hour out of your mythical life to chill with some hippy kids? Thank you, thank you...can we come to your house because we don't have anywhere else to go."

In some recordings you'll hear their baby crying in the background because they want a fruitsnack. You might hear a motorcycle drive by from outside. Every recording is different. We aren't professionals by any means. We bring a certain heart and soul to the literary world that we felt was often lacking in these money-backed things (which I love but I love us more).

MM: *If the GOD OF THINGS HENCE came to you in the form of*

a boxelder bug and asked, job-interview style, "Where do yourself five years from now?" what would say about The Knox House? Will you still be recording poets? Will you have expanded? Will you become a nonprofit? Will you expand services? How will the world have changed because of you? Tell us what you see in your crystal ball.

SC: In five years I know we'll still be building annexes onto the House. I don't know that I'll ever be able to devote such expansive lengths of time to travel around and finding writers (which honestly, Emily and Bryce did most of), but I know Emily plans to keep looking for money from wherever she can to devote her life to this. I think, right now, we're all at this point where we want to see what the world has to offer to each of us, individually. But you never know. I'm sure I will keep recording people wherever I end up and sending them back to Emily or Bryce to add to the website. At this point, our seed hasn't even broke soil. If, when, I, Bryce, maybe even Emily take a backseat, I'm sure there will be younger kids ready and willing to pick up the mantle. I do think we are going to have a significant impact in the world (of literature? Of everything?). We are pretty dope kids that did a pretty dope project, at least that's what people tell us, and I think that the personal nature of this project is going to resonate with the people that were a part of it or that just stumble upon it. People can sit in their beds and listen to writers from New Orleans and see how their writing differs from people in Connecticut. That's not something that was as easy as it is now with our contribution to the written world.

MM: *What about The Knox Writers' House lifeblood, i.e., you as an individual person—what are you up to? Striving for? Thinking about? Making? Selling? Studying? Writing? Doing? Give us a glimpse into the reality show you call your life.*

SC: Right now I'm at this point in my life post-college where I finally don't feel panicked about everything. I'm mentally at a place where I can look at my past present and future and feel good about everything, despite being in my mom's basement currently (shit that sounds bad). I'm applying to grad school right now because I really do want to become the best writer I possibly can, and I'm a kid that needs that immediate community and pressure to make strides as a writer. I'm got this pretty chill job at a bookstore that allows me ample time to take whatever little money I make and travel around (Portland and North Carolina and Connecticut have been my most recent). I've become obsessed with podcasts like WTF with Marc Maron and Bill Simmons' BS Report, so I've really been contemplating making my own podcast along those veins (hopefully one day replacing Jimmy Fallon late night, HA). I've been writing a lot more these past couple months than I did in the few months immediately after graduating, which I'm super pleased about. Lot of flash fictions, and one longer short story I'm almost done with. Basically, I'm chillin pretty hard and planning a move to New Orleans in the near future.

MM: *And you're moving to the Twin Cities when?*

SC: Hahahah, man. I will say, "sometime in the future." I've been in the Midwest for the better part of 22 years, so right now I'm pretty deadset at getting the hell out, though I do love it. I'm looking south right now, with New Orleans being my dream landing spot. I need to avoid winter for at least a while to recharge my batteries. But I've long held the belief that if and when I move back to the Midwest, the Twin Cities are at the top of the list. I've never met someone from that place that I don't love and there's more culture there than almost anywhere else in the country. And you guys have pretty great hip-hop, which is a huge plus for me. Keep a couch open for us.

BECAUSE A FATHER IS LIKE A GOD

for Crys

I bow to the river
   hauling itself
      headlong into a narrow gorge

I bow to waterfalls cascading
   over polished walls of rock
those steep unstable slopes

I bow to the falling curtain of rain
the habits of perception
      to that belt of blue-needled spruce

I bow to the years I walked
   the ridge's knife-edge path
      without you

Because a father is like a god
   and a god is always filled
      with power he dispenses

I bow to the plummeting ravines
   the perilous spine of cliffs
      every cloud-wrapped cave

Hemmed in by a protruding
   granite slab on one side
      a foaming cauldron on the other

I bow
   to the world unfallen
      when you died

To the gun shot
    exploding through thorn bushes
      and towering thistle

Suspended between earth and sky
between drifting mist
    and precipitous drop

I bow to Rilke's angels
    who break us open
      out of who we are

I bow to the one who divides
who will and who will not
be refined by suffering

On this gravel mat
    clapped against
      a limestone ledge

I bow as I always do
    to the crumbling temple
I made of you

James Cihlar

Unembarrassed Poetry

"No ideas but in things," William Carlos Williams wrote. As writers, editors, and teachers we're familiar with the catchy bromide, "show, don't tell." Must it really be one or the other? Are our choices that binary? On further investigation, it may seem that the past one-hundred-plus years of poetics offers a bewildering set of alternatives. From W.H. Auden's socially motivated definition of poetry as "memorable speech" to John Ashbery's modeling of the technique of collage, anyone writing or reading poetry now has access to a grab bag of strategies. If poets by definition create their own methodologies, an engine that works itself in their poetry, getting their readers from point A to point B, what exceptions are permitted by the rules?

Before we can even get to that question, we have to address the misconceptions of poetry as elitist and unpopular. Too often, poets are placed on the defensive in American culture. I once worked at a nonprofit literary press where the accountant argued that we should abandon publishing poetry because it "didn't sell" and we "didn't make money off of it." Okay, it's one thing for an accountant to say that, but when it turned out she was repeating a line from the board of directors, I had to scratch my head. What happened to being mission-driven? When poetry is habitually placed on square one, justifying its existence, no wonder that those who care about discussing the finer points of poetics acquire the air of elitism.

While listening to Joy Harjo perform with her group Poetic Justice at the Association of Writers and Writing Programs Conference in 2010 the notion of a poetry that is neither apologetic nor embarrassed presented itself. Sitting near the front of a full and appreciative crowd, I experienced full-on the many voices of a poet in performance. From jazz-inspired tributes to Charlie Parker in "Bird" to direct quotes of a country western song in "Deer Dancer" to her own distinctive, incantatory voice in "She Had Some Horses," Harjo was fearless in her presentation, "a woman who is gorgeously intelligent" ("The Real Revolution Is Love"). Why shouldn't a Native American poet play the saxophone? Who's to say an artist can express herself in only one mode? No explanations or justifications were necessary. One of the things that stood out was Harjo's ability to offer, in the midst of the richness and complexity of each journey her poems took, a simple, direct, unassuming, even unembarrassed statement of meaning—whether it was a two lines from a song by Kenny Rogers, an aside to the audience, or the recognition of shared experience captured in a refrain.

It seems to me that there is a rich tradition of plain speech, unadorned expression, in contemporary poetry. Of course, it's hard to claim comprehensiveness when my examples are my favorites—Joy Harjo, Elizabeth Bishop, James Wright, Sylvia Plath, and Theodore Roethke. Admittedly, this is a random grouping, but I hope an examination of individual poems will lead to some clarity about the term. Unembarrassed Poets as a group may embrace diverse styles but they are defined by their willingness to simply state what they mean sometimes, to depart from the script, to break the fourth wall, to offer an unflattering self-admission in their poems, leading to a further connection with the reader.

Although Elizabeth Bishop, for instance, takes William Carlos Williams' advice to heart in her detail-laden poem "Little Exercise," providing a cascade of image upon image, describing a tropical storm as a dog looking for a bed to lie down in, or mangrove roots resembling "fistfuls of limp fish skeletons," near the end she offers the simple statement, "It is raining there." No, really? If we hadn't figured that out yet, we weren't paying attention. And yet, the line comes as a relief to the reader, a welcome instance of pure voice. Perhaps only in poetry, with its origin in the oral tradition, its lineage of "memorable speech" can we appreciate a statement of the obvious not as a redundancy—as it would be in prose—but as a pronouncement—oracular. It feels processional, as if, while we march through the poet's improvised litany together, we naturally arrive at the moment when she bestows a blessing.

This prayer offers the comfort of affirming our relationship to place: It is raining there. Understood—there is a time for every purpose under heaven.

James Wright's poems are similarly unapologetic in subject matter and unembarrassed in tone. In "To a Blossoming Pear Tree," he uses the Romantic convention of an ode to nature to "tell you something, / Something human." A century or more after Wordsworth, he amplifies the call to present the common plight in common terms. On the snowbound streets of Minneapolis an old man propositions Wright: "Give it to me, he begged. / I'll pay you anything." Nothing could be more outwardly further from and inwardly closer to "the spontaneous overflow of powerful feelings" defined in *Lyrical Ballads*. Perhaps Modernism is Romanticism squared.

Wright should have copyrighted the "pow" ending, which he supplies in poem after poem, coupling surprise and simplicity to great effect. For instance, in "Northern Pike" and "Lying in a Hammock at William Duffy's Farm in Pine Island, Minnesota" the last lines are more than understatement; they ignite the preceding lines retroactively. Largely accessible, "Northern Pike" nevertheless contains some idiosyncratic lines understandable only to Wright— what's the relevance of the "right-hand wrist of my cousin who is a policeman"? That stumbling block would matter more if not for the clarity of the last line: "I am so happy." I first encountered Wright's deft use of plain speech in an Introduction to Creative Writing class at the University of Iowa, when my instructor Cathleen Michaels showed us "Lying in a Hammock." Her point was that we must "earn" the right to make plain, powerful statements, by "grounding" a poem in specifics. Twenty-five years later, I taught the same poem in an upper-level American Poetry literature class at the University of Minnesota, where we admired Wright's ability to express the thoughts and feelings of the individual in lyric verse by recording the sensory impressions of a moment, a traditionally Romantic approach, followed by the decidedly Modernistic or Post-Modernistic distilled statement of the truth: "I have wasted my life." Wright's directness sends us scurrying back to the start of what we had assumed at first to be a typical pastoral, a pleasantly bucolic lyric. How did we get to this ending, and why does it feel so right? On rereading we see the darkness embedded in the imagery: the butterfly's wings are ruffled by the wind—a sign of transience that undercuts the permanence of bronze, the adjective Wright first used to describe its color. The bird floating overhead is a chicken hawk, not a dove or an eagle. And what are those golden stones blazing in the sun? Oh right, they are "The droppings of last year's horses." Unembarrassment was there all along.

Not only Wright's poems show that the stock caveat against abstractions should be amended. Theodore Roethke's "The Waking" showcases the power of simple statement embedded within a complicated structure. The villanelle is made up of six stanzas, the first five of three lines in an a/b/a and the last of four lines in an a/b/a/a rhyme scheme. The first and third lines of the first stanza alternatingly repeat at the end of each stanza, with both repeating at the end. Got that? For those who've tried, it's hard enough to get a poem in this form to make sense, let alone to be moving. When Roethke arrives at the simple statement, "I should know," at the end of the first line of the last stanza, it is supported by the rhyme scheme and the form, but it also reads as powerful indicator of character and mood.

Sylvia Plath's "Mirror" shows the power of plain speech in a persona poem. Plath's poem is a tour de force of imagery, written from the perspective of a household object. This unconventional perspective allows the poet to present timeworn images in fresh language, colored by character: the woman who lives in this house "turns to those liars, the candles or the moon." Even the "terrible fish" of the lake of the mirror at the end of the poem, easily resonant with the unconscious, is one more rich detail in this tick list of refashioned images. So when we hit the short, declarative sentence, "I am important to her," in the fourth-to-last line, it's like a cool drink of water in a hot, dark, close room. It reminds me of another line, "I live here," in Plath's densely mythic "The Moon and the Yew Tree." Such lines, occurring when and where they do, deriving their effects from context as much as from content, have the power that Adrienne Rich describes in "Cartographies of Silence":

> if from time to time I long to turn
>
> like the Eleusinian hierophant
> holding up a simple ear of grain . . .

More than jokes, slang, or simple sentences, Unembarrassed Poetry offers the surprise of eternal truth about the human character and the world via plain but charged speech embedded in lyric description, litany, persona, form, or collage.

Unembarrassed Poetry is at least two things: lyric poetry full of sensory details and complex images; simple, direct statements that may reveal the poet's vulnerability. The manner in which an Unembarrassed Poet turns the corner between these two things, bridges them, slips in the surprise, is key to the poem's effectiveness. Otherwise, it is just flat language. Context is everything. Perhaps another familiar definition of poetry, this one from Emily Dickinson, is apt here. She said, "If I feel physically as if the top of my head were taken off, I know *that* is poetry." She's right in focusing on the way poetry makes us *feel*. If we all did that, maybe we could sidestep the banal preconceptions about poetry's elitism, unpopularity, and unprofitability. Any art that can pull *this* off has got to be worth something—because we're going to want to keep feeling it again and again.

Works Consulted

Joy Harjo, *How We Became Human: New and Selected Poems: 1975—2001*, Norton, 2002.

Stephen Greenblatt, editor, *The Norton Anthology of English Literature*, Norton, 2006.

X.J. Kennedy and Dana Gioia, editors, *Literature: An*

Introduction to Fiction, Poetry, Drama, and Writing,
Longman, 2010.

Sylvia Plath, *Ariel*, Harper, 1961.

Sylvia Plath, *Crossing the Water*, Harper & Row, 1971.

Adrienne Rich, *The Dream of a Common Language*,
Norton, 1978.

James Wright, *Above the River: The Complete Poems*, Wesleyan
University Press, 1990.

ONE MAYBE YOU'LL KEEP

Dear Reluctant Sportsman,
maybe you'll release one
into the watery teeth of the wilds,
a tiny capillary
of our great circulatory system.

Dear Familiar Face
in the Passenger Seat,
I saw you undressing
that comely cornfield. I agree.
Maybe we're more alike
than even our combustible
engines suggest, and if we are,
you hope the next truckstop
has a wedge of pie
to die for too.

Dear Cell Phone Radiation,
we arrive almost invisibly
on the threshold of distant
relatives like a secret cold front,
but our departure demands
much horn honking and
happy hands waving
all the way
to the end
of the on ramp.
Our relief,
an algorithm
of how lonely
company makes us.

Dear Rainbow Trout,
you're a pretty fish

and I wish we lived
near the shivering brook
and the sunken tree,
then maybe we wouldn't forget
how to leave.

Morgan Grayce Willow

Two Roberts and a Picasso, or How I Became a Poet

One by one we enter the classroom, girls in skirts and boys in slacks and shirt with collar as required by the college dress code. At the entrance just inside the door stands the professor wearing his tweed suit and tie, his shoes polished to a high shine. As each student files by he greets us. "Good morning, Mr. Smith." "Good morning Miss Peterson." As I walk by this particular late fall Monday, he breaks tradition and says, "Now, wasn't that fun?"

Excruciatingly shy in my first semester at a small liberal arts college in the middle of Iowa, I feel my face burn and am unable to utter even the obligatory, "Good morning, Dr. Kildahl." I do, however, know without a doubt what he refers to: my first real attempt at writing a poem.

Truth be told, I hadn't meant to write a poem and wouldn't have dared to call it that at the time. In looking back, I see that's what it was, though it's just as well I don't have it to read now. I'm sure my current critical eye would judge it a poor specimen. At the time, however, I felt a secret joy welling up between shyness and relief. I hadn't, after all, failed the week's assignment.

I was enrolled in an interdisciplinary honor's class combining the study of art, literature and philosophy. Every week, we were required to write what Dr. Kildahl called a reaction paper, a five-page (or so) essay responding to lectures, reading assignments, and discussions. The handwritten essays were always due in Friday morning's class. This meant that every Thursday night I'd be up after the ten o'clock curfew – and usually after my roommates and I had returned from our regular jaunt to the student union for the sundae we fondly called a Brownie Goop, its hot fudge melting a trail through vanilla ice cream and down to a gooey brownie layer at bottom. Each Thursday all semester long I'd faithfully written the essay and turned it in on time. But on that one particular Thursday evening, I was simply not in the mood to do the week's homework. Instead, my gaze lingered on a poster hanging in my dorm room. I responded to it in short sentences and brief, descriptive phrases, with line breaks. The poster was Picasso's "Old Guitarist."

The previous summer after my 1967 high school graduation, I had worked in Chicago as a nanny. My farm upbringing among numerous younger siblings, nephews, and neighbor kids in need of babysitters made me well qualified in the eyes of my new employers to care for an eighteen-month-old boy. To me, it meant a chance to get off the farm and into the city to experience culture and the arts. Each week, I had one day off. On every one of them, I took the bus to the El and rode downtown to the Art Institute. In addition to the Institute's remarkable collection of Impressionist art (which I would learn about the following fall in Kildahl's class) and a Surrealism exhibition, it also happened that the Institute was showing a retrospective of Pablo Picasso's work. Every week I wandered among the galleries, pacing myself to savor the art, to take it in bit by bit. Then one day I turned the corner into a small gallery showing work from Picasso's blue period. There in the center of the longest wall hung Picasso's "Old Guitarist" painted in 1903. I was transfixed. Though there were other paintings from the period in the room, I saw none of them. I was deeply moved by the guitarist's blue crossed legs, the angle of his shoulder and neck, his languid fingers over the sound hole of the guitar, the clasp of the guitarist's other hand high up on the fret board in the shadows. My feet seemed to sink through the marble floor.

For the rest of the summer, I spent time each week in Picasso's blue period room with the Old Guitarist. I knew the poster in the gift shop could not truly replicate the way the brush strokes in the painting reflected light or capture the shifts in value among the blues and greens. Yet, I had to have it. I bought the print to hang in my dorm room come fall. It was "The Old Guitarist" who became the subject of my "failed" essay assignment in Dr. Kildahl's class, and my first poem. His simple remark, "Now, wasn't that fun," as well as the "A" on the paper when he handed it back, affirmed for me that whatever it was I'd done, it had value.

I kept that early, handwritten poem for many years, its lined pages becoming more brittle with each move, the many boxes of papers, poems and journals accumulating with alarming speed. Eventually however, it vanished. Years later I would read with wonder Wallace Stevens' poem "The Man with the Blue Guitar," believed by many to be a response to the same Picasso painting. While my poem had been primarily descriptive, an attempt to sketch the painting for a reader, Stevens used the image to create a kind of fugue that illustrates how art and poetry interact with reality. Nevertheless, his opening lines always remind me of my earliest poem:

> The man bent over his guitar,
> A shearsman of sorts. The day was green.
>
> They said, "You have a blue guitar,
> You do not play things as they are."
>
> The man replied, "Things as they are
> Are changed upon the blue guitar."

In his thirty-three part poem, Stevens demonstrates that the musician – and by inference, the artist or poet – transforms things in the act of creating. In the painting, everything is blue <u>except</u> the guitar. In my case, I was the "thing" transformed by the painting and, in turn, by my poem. Dr. Kildahl's response to it, gave me permission to believe I could be a poet.

* * *

Fast forward to 1970. I've hitchhiked out West and now live in southern California. Too late for San Francisco's summer of love, I've become something of a weekend hippie. I commute by car to an office job during the week, but on weekends, I travel by thumb. I hitch rides to beaches up and down the coast or to go hiking in the San Bernardino

Mountains or Anza-Borrego Desert. By now, I've accumulated a folder jammed full of pages and pages of poems. One or two have been published in very small literary magazines. I'm taking poetry seriously and wanting to learn more about it, but not in a position to take classes. From library copies of *Poetry Magazine*, I've discovered Robert Duncan. I remember having a copy of *Bending the Bow*, from New Directions (1968), though not whether it was a borrowed library copy or one I owned.

Duncan's language had me mesmerized. I was captivated by the mystery of the *Passages* series, though I didn't understand any of it. I had no idea how to enter these layered poems, yet their sound and splashes of mythology drew me back again and again. My preparation for poetry of this kind had come in two parts. First, in sophomore high school English class, Mrs. Gilles had introduced us to Greek mythology. And then there had been Dr. Kildahl. For his class, I'd given a presentation on T. S. Eliot's "The Love Song of J. Alfred Prufrock." I'd had the advantage of editorial notations and critical essays to help me figure out the references and guide me through interpretations of the poem. Now, however, outside academia, I was on my own with Robert Duncan's poems. So I simply read and reread, listening to the rhythms, noticing the accumulation of images. From the title poem, "Bending the Bow":

> We've our business to attend Day's duties,
> bend back the bow in dreams as we may
> till the end rimes in the taut string
> with the sending.

I gathered Duncan was writing about writing the poem even as he was engaged in writing the poem. In graduate school some ten years later, I would come to understand the Moderns' determined focus on the process of creating a whole new poetics. But at that time, despite my utter lack of context for Duncan's layerings of time, space and poetics, I was bedazzled by the headiness of his poems. His conceptual meanderings were grounded on the page for me by his erratic

patterns of line break, indentations, and spacing. In "The Fire –
Passages 13," for example, the first stanza (if it can even be called
a stanza) consists of a grid of words – six across by six down –
stripped from the shape of sentence syntax. Two lines follow:

jump	stone	hand	leaf	shadow	sun
day	plash	coin	light	downstream	fish

Duncan's work was rattling all my preconceptions about how
poems should be shaped, what they could be about, how they
should sound. Long before my introduction to Gertrude Stein or
the language poets, I'd found someone for whom language could
be a plastic medium, a poetry in which words could be isolated and
recombined in the way Renoir broke up light and recombined it to
create a different kind of whole.

And yet at the same time, there was Duncan's concern for the
social context. In "The Multiversity," he takes on the subject of the
Free Speech Movement at the University of California, Berkeley,
only a few years earlier. Here, Duncan's pastiche of language
embraces the direct prose of the newspaper article:

false news: 1) that the students broke into Sproul's office,
    vandalizing, creating disorder; 2) that the Free Speech
    Movement has no wide support, only an irresponsible min-
    ority going on strike

Here was a poet who, it seemed to me, could have his head in the
clouds and his feet on the ground at the same time.

* * *

"Are you enjoying the class? Do you feel like you're getting
something out of it?"

The speaker towers above my desk, standing at the corner from
which the credenza for my IBM Selectric typewriter extends. Tall,
broad shouldered and barrel chested, poet Robert Peters gazes
down at me. He holds in his hands some papers I've just typed for

him. Quietly, I reply, "Yes, I am."

The class he refers to is his poetry workshop in the MFA program at UC, Irvine, where he's on the faculty and I've come to work as a secretary for the department. It's 1971, and I'm in my trying-to-go-straight phase after my hippie years. It's been difficult to tame my wild, long hair, and even more difficult to trade in loose, wide-bottomed pants and sandals for dresses, sling-back shoes and panty hose in order to dress appropriately for the office. Among the faculty in the department, Robert Peters has been one of the warmest and most welcoming. Perhaps it was the Midwest connection, for, when asked, I'd told him I'd come to California from Iowa. He'd explained that he was originally from Wisconsin.

Peters had observed that, on rainy days, I often took my lunch break in the department's poetry library. On the more frequent sunny days, I borrowed books from that library and sat among the bottle brush, agapanthus, and bougainvillea at one of the many benches throughout the park-like campus. Of my secretarial duties, my favorite was the cataloging of books and journals for the poetry library. At first, I'd felt both thrilled and overwhelmed by the floor-to-ceiling shelves filled with poetry books of all shapes and sizes parading all the way around the room. But gradually I came to recognize poets' names and book titles. Of course, I'd begun my orientation by reading work by the faculty which, in addition to Peters, included Charles Wright. When Peters learned that I liked to write poetry, he very generously invited me to sit in on the workshop.

The problem was that I was still very shy. I also lacked experience with creative writing workshops, despite an intro to writing poetry class I'd had during a brief stint at the University of Iowa. The class had been taught by a student (whose name I don't remember) in The Workshop. We'd done virtually no peer feedback and had only the instructor's opinion of our drafts to work with while writing poems. As a result, during Peters' weekly workshop meetings, I was consistently tongue-tied. I read all the poems other poets turned in and marked them with care, but I couldn't bring myself to speak in class unless called upon, which was not

Peters' teaching style. I also had not, as I'd hoped, been inspired to write lots of poems. On the contrary, though I'd turned in a couple of poems for feedback, my use of language felt stilted. I was unable to access what I most wanted in those poem drafts, which made me even more hesitant to share my work.

Nevertheless, though I was unable to articulate it to Robert Peters, I was learning a great deal from the poems written by the other students, from his commentary on them, and from the students' feedback for each other. He encouraged me to continue coming for the remainder of the semester and to participate to whatever degree I felt comfortable. Since I was auditing the course, there would be no grade to document a failure, whatever I might feel about my success in the workshop. I wanted to learn the craft of poetry and to expand my capabilities with the language. At that point, I did so primarily by absorption.

Compression of language was the goal then. The ideal workshop poem appeared to be a swift progress through discernible narrative tightly wound around a few spare images. Peters' own "The Sow's Head," the title poem from his 1968 collection, modeled the aesthetic well:

> The day was like pewter.
> The gray lake a coat
> open at the throat.
>
> . . . .
>
> I passed the iodine-colored brook
> hard waters open
> the weight of the sow's head
> an ache from shoulder to waist,
> the crook of my elbow numb;
>
> . . . .
>
> I was wrong to take it.

. . . .

> It sat on the snow
> as though it lived below,
> leviathan come for air

I wanted my poems to sound like his, or like this one written
by Linda Burnham, one of the students in the workshop, which
appeared in *Synapse*, the student literary magazine, under the
title "At the Reading":

> He held irony like walnuts
> in his cheeks.
> There were parentheses
> around his mouth,
> ravines of disappointment.
> He used his eyes like periods of pain.

However, I had just learned, from Robert Duncan, how to open
out my lines, how to get space into the poem.

I did overcome my shyness enough to submit at least one
poem to the workshop. There may have been more, but I recall
one in particular because I have documentation of it. The
poetry editor of *Synapse*, who was also in the workshop, found
enough in the poem to like that he invited me to submit it to the
magazine. I was pleased, since *Synapse* seemed a cut above the
little magazines in which my poems had appeared before. After
revisions, I submitted "Reading a Novel."

> Reading a novel
>   on Sunday afternoon
> only makes Sunday afternoon
>   more like Sunday afternoon.
> The characters
>   whom I've come to know too well
> are suspended from the ceiling,

and I bump into them as I move about the empty room which
  by this time
is getting overcrowded with impressions
        and reflections
                        and introspections
and memories.
Hard to remain quiet
  when the careening images funnel in my ears
and it's hard to be alone with so much company.

Reading this poem now, I recognize the naiveté and lack of imagery common to the work of beginning poets. Yet, it is for my beginning that this essay gives thanks. To two Roberts – Duncan and Peters. To Picasso. And to Dr. Kildahl. May I have the vision and generosity to nurture beginnings for those poets who cross my own path, as he did for me.

Sarah Fox

ECLIPSE

now that white horse slipping past my garden gate   it's night   torn fever & an old blood
lb coming loose down where sea rocks mix up with asbestos   I thought a glint of it
tarnished glass   old truck windshield   thought that might serrate the bloodpouch   stab a straight
ur   not clot   it's like a medieval bladderbag book-bind   secret bosomed book   bladders
om dead cows   or   the family horse back when days had less frenzy   one or two measures
ep up step down   ("clop-clop")   buried families mixed in with all the truck parts and asphalt
the garden   & with hoof sluff   Not to say I spy   tangible flank / silk nostril / hay-jammed chops
if the white horse slipped in noisily   bled into the garden bed stepping everywhere on shards
here taillights and heirloom mirrors sifted under   The garden has ghosts like doll closets do
aybe it's moonshadow   I want to get at it   the bulb down there   A Medicine Man
ld me *go get it if a horse comes for you ride him out you're permitted*   Tell Me Dear   a horse
ot white) once I loved her   my father did too   he took me out to the stables   once
ell off   stirrup-stuck   scaled jump poles   dangle-brained   my father agape   maybe scared
rses are like bears   don't run after them or spook just stand still there   Hold on I'll get
u he said   I was almost fielded I thought   a goner   He pulled out his black bag its squeeze-click
uckle scuffed up   roll of gauze tape hemostat stethoscope & stuff   sometimes I'd find
up on a shelf smell the leather dust   I got back on the horse   Later on a birth run I took
e girl's placenta out to the orchid stacks   pale yellow bloom underleaf   took the placenta
tside in a pail   some kids helped dig a hole   Hmong moms root the placenta where it lands
pull a soul back to its Go   [*what's soul*]   maybe glass   white horse   a glint or blood pouch   hope
est (placenta)   food at either threshold   "soul dowry"   Other medicines too stored for later
a ghost or not   or maybe bagged   The Medicine Man said *lift it up   don't tear in don't eat*
ything   *Maybe* he said *maybe that bulb has dyskinesia   could be shaky after such a spell* mixed up
ith garden dirt   frazzled root hairs plum pits   We had put that blood bulb to cure   (like tobacco)
ven glass and vehicle metal & the old guy who built the place his shaved off whisker bits
robably in there   *You know what it's for* he said not "saying" like normal but in a dream way
owing as hand sequence and dialectic modes via eyes & mouth ("wizened") He keeps changing
s garb even   destabilizes age   if he's wearing furs the medicine means LAY ALONG THE BODY'S
FT SIDE HOLD ITS HAND   but if I get to him on the quiltbacks of turtles he's fixing to school me
pulse theory or substratum nomenclature which is the same as doorways   He's a house call   Once
om his province he said *here's the head of a fox taking the shape of your own head*   I felt
allooning around my ears but he was the one he had furs   my heart's on the left   as all are
e got ink dark and lay flat then he was laying flat inside my skin leaning against my inside
arts but not to squirt out   this was the schooling LISTEN but that really means
FEEL SOMETHING which is the same as TO SEE   I saw that Medicine Man say ("be") FATHER
t it was really a reflection   It was my own father crept a part of himself unto my safekeeping long
o in my child time must've   Turtles live a long time shouldering their domicile everywhere   My father
e still flesh one (just barely) he's just barely my very very dying father   husk of him hobbles
the church aisle mouthing "How Great Thou Art" all wavery all crooked step up step down
ead hung sickness low   Encased debris of a careless wager   anger taken up   ancestral geyser
ot up in him spewed out everywhere CLUSTER-BOMBED   Even his heart hardly works
ried pouch drained   brittle   What black bag I don't remember that he said   I'm
pposed to find the medicine   A white horse signaled me to come over   I had never

seen that white horse my Medicine Man is not imaginary & as father they're the same Lab
coat, seal fur Unbinding my garden steeps a heart patch making it apricot fragrant for him
and when a hoof cracks through bursts it up liquid dirt basin as in baptismal I'm to lay in
there and not forget he said *you don't have to forget* Once a little like this two hands made a bowl
(each hand a father on one father's body) stared hard to see who it was I was he really really loved it

Regan Smith

The Poet in my Office Keeps Writing me Death Threats

The poet in my office keeps writing me death threats. Last week it was a disembowelment epitaph in iambic pentameter. Yesterday, an asphyxiation haiku.

"Thad," I say to him when he stops in the break room for a bowl of Hot Cheetos from the Cheeto bar. "This is really getting out of control. My wife's threatening to call the cops."

"I have absolutely no *idea* what you're talking about," Thad replies, and tears open a package of microwaved nacho cheese.

On Fridays, Thad tapes a flier for his weekly poetry reading on the break room door. On Mondays, he stops by each cubicle, asking people what they did over the weekend. Usually we lie, tell him the kids were sick, some relatives were in town, Coors Light was 2/$10 at Safeway. But last month I decided to be honest and told Thad I just wasn't that into poetry. The next day there was a syphilis sonnet taped to my Tupperware of ambrosia salad.

Sometimes Thad's death threats are a true work of art, and I wish that I had just gone to see the guy read once or twice. And sometimes, Thad gets lazy.

I will nail your balls / to the walls / motherfucker he inscribed on my favorite urinal.

My wife, Amy, has taken to stealing the poems from my dresser and making photocopies at Kinko's. She compiles them in a three-ringer binder labeled "Case Study Two: Thad Threats." Case Study One materialized after she watched an entire season of *Cheaters* on DVD and developed an obsession with our neighbor's late night dog walking.

"New one on my urinal today," I text Amy.

"pics???" she texts back.

After my screensaver starts flashing photoshopped images of me being mauled by polar bears, I decide I've had enough. On Friday night I tell Amy to load up her Robitussin purse with the 'Tussin Flask and we drive over to the Flick 'n' Sip Café.

Thad's reading is short and surprisingly moving, an allegory about baby ducklings and loss of innocence, and afterward we walk up to him to say hi and offer tissues.

"Hey, that was really good, man," I say.

"Would you mind smudging your finger print on this glass?" Amy asks.

Thad thanks us, takes a tissue, and we head home.

That Monday when I get into work there is a ham on my desk and a limerick written in orange lettering taped to my monitor. I put the ham in my knapsack and crawl under the desk. After making sure nobody's watching I hold the paper under my nose, inhale deeply, and let the scent of Hot Cheetos totally fucking take over me.

BARELY A SKYLINE

There perhaps is a kind of loss within the hotel   But yes this is
A doorway into the river

Day rippling over brick where the ditch is a bright slash

A few leaves left at the edge of reason   Open
To a slow sunlight

Sucking mouth berthed at the side so the way light moves
Might be a set of tubes over all the white walls

A freakishly wincing predator
Tears at the breast   Above the rain-filled street

Man-up on a park bench
Understand that dress blinking in the sun

Leslie Adrienne Miller

Some Thoughts on Privacy, Poetry and the Unwelcome Reader

When she won the Pulitzer, poet Rita Dove remarked that it was like having the door thrown open while you're on the john. She was hardly unknown at the time, but the prize suddenly expanded her audience from literary circles to popular ones. Poet William Matthews once quipped that the phrase "famous poet" is an oxymoron. In other words, being a poet and being well known are generally mutually exclusive conditions, so the privacy that comes with obscurity is easy to get used to over the 10-20 years it often takes to build a literary reputation and readership. But if your work suddenly leaps the boundaries of literary circles to become more widely known, your privacy diminishes, and so does your freedom to maintain an easy intimacy with the reader.

Privacy in poetry is a little bit like privacy in Facebook: it's a useful illusion, and most of us don't adequately imagine who or what might be interested in invading that privacy—corporate interests, stalkers, or just plain opportunists looking to attach themselves to someone with a little more literary legitimacy. It's very difficult and time consuming to figure out how to manage it, and once you do, you're still not really protected because even if you know who all your "friends" are, you don't know what friends' friends might be doing with your information. It's all about who has access to your information, and how easily an unwelcome stranger can use it for purposes you never intended.

It's all well and good when your reader is a decent person with some shared values, maybe even someone who knows you personally and well, better yet a writer friend who enters into your work with an open mind and heart. But who among us can prevent the relative stranger from reinventing us for their own purposes? Who among us can prevent the misogynist blogger, the conservative relative, disgruntled student, crusty administrator, or volatile stranger from waltzing into a poem's vivid and intimate moment and suddenly deforming it with the context of the new point of view?

There is where your privacy ends: precisely where the reader's life enters your text and distorts it into something you no longer recognize as yours. Few of us imagine this reader when we are writing our poems. In fact, if we did fully and constantly imagine this reader, we would not write at all, yet understanding the unwelcome reader can ultimately make us, if not stronger writers, then at least writers who have a more complex understanding of audience.

The unwelcome reader isn't always vindictive; more often, he's just a naive reader, some lost undergrad who has an assignment, or an inexperienced reviewer trying to build a portfolio. Pinning your work to whatever biographical details he can find might be the only way he knows. He has just enough to be dangerous, and whatever he does say is certainly more about him than about you or your work. But here's the rub: He has just as much, if not more, chance of showing up in a Google search (and of being quoted by the next naive reader) as a thoughtful review in a literary journal.

This is a subject full of maddening paradoxes:

Paradox 1: The only privacy you do have as a poet (beyond not publishing at all) comes largely from the fact that so few people read poetry, and those who do read poetry are often well schooled in literary critical history of the last hundred years, so they know better than to equate writer and speaker.

Paradox 2: If it's true, as Richard A. Lanham suggests in *The Economics of Attention: Style and Substance in the Age of Information* that attention is what is in short supply and that ways of getting it are themselves the locus of value in present culture, then self-promotion for poets becomes paradoxically both an essential and potentially damaging activity: if you and your work are suddenly everywhere at once, ubiquitous, you may easily diminish your value, while the rare and hard to find might command attention by its intriguing exclusivity.

Paradox 3: There are two opposing strategies for maintaining privacy in a literary life: you can reveal much less of the self in your work-- which might involve hiding behind more artifice, or you can reveal so much that you will bury the reader in an avalanche of details, many of which are redundant, quotidian, and just plain dull, so that sorting it all to get the choice bits becomes a Promethean task most readers won't care to take on (think Ginsberg). This is the confessional/ anticonfessional divide. Think Rachel Zucker vs Ange Mlinko. As a writer, when you choose one end of this spectrum or the other, you have to remember that you are also choosing your readers! And the more numerous readers who expect intimacies from poets are not often the same few who expect artifice.

Most readers find and want to find autobiography in poetry even where there is none or merely some. You can hem and haw all you want about naive readers confusing speaker and writer, but the truth is that even reviewers still conflate author and speaker in poems, especially in online and newspaper reviews where wider audiences are courted and "personal interest" is a selling point.

Paradox 4: The more skilled you are as a writer at putting your reader in a situation, idea or complex of these without being overly sentimental or melodramatic, the more danger the reader will assume the experience rendered in writing is real or autobiographical. If sentiment has to be shoveled into or onto the poem by the writer, the reader is less likely to assume the authenticity of the experience and start poking around for the "you" in it.

Paradox 5: If you "play" with your reader's sense of the truth with meta-poetry (stepping out of the frame to address the reader directly with instructions on how to read you), you risk pissing them off because you've intruded on their assumption that they were already inside your mind and your life.

Paradox 6: The more you obfuscate to try to protect your

privacy, the more the reader will suspect you are hiding yourself and, therefore, the harder the reader may try to "read" the invisible you in the poem.

Paradox 7: In a stylistic sense, the more "literary" your work is, the more distance you put between yourself and your readers. The more you trade heavily in literary devices like aesthetic distance, sonic devices, verbal play, lyric compression, allusion and elliptical syntax, the more your audience shrinks to an in-the-know few. You have ever greater privacy—and obscurity. You escape media attention because local media outlets won't have reviewers willing or able to contextualize work they can't penetrate by pinning it to a personality. And if your publisher can't sell the "you" in your work, you are probably consigning yourself to very small presses who serve intrepid lovers of the difficult.

And some observations:
If you are a female writer, you are more likely to be read as an autobiographical one because female experience is still generally equated with personal experience, while male experience is more often regarded as universal.

How much print footprint do you have? How much digital footprint do you have? Either way, your reader will draw a skewed portrait based on the available public details, which may appear to be important because they are public, because they are repeated, and/or because they have aroused strong negative emotion in a reader. You do not and cannot control which of this information becomes magnified in the public sphere, but negatives have a sneaky way of replicating faster than positives. Things said in praise of you may be used to mock you and vice versa. Readers will take and respond to what they think they understand and ignore the rest.

I'm not sure myself exactly how to balance all of the above, but I do know that in imagining your own unwelcome reader, in acknowledging he exists and might not mean you well, you are already inhabiting a different position from which to view your own experiences as fodder for poems. Who is your least welcome reader, and why is he so unwelcome at the table of your work ? What does he assume that you do not wish him to assume? What does he expect of you that you refuse to deliver in your work? What does he expect of you that you can't help delivering in your work? Why is he even interested in your work, and what does he gain from misreading you? How might you play with or off of his unwelcome reading of your work and/or your life?

Your unwelcome reader will not be mine, but a composite personality or group attracted to and propelled by some confluence of elements unique to your own writing. At the very least, knowing he's listening could make you a more inventive writer. Think of Eastern European poets like Vasko Popa or Zbigniew Herbert inventing clever ways to simultaneously mock political figures and escape the censorship of their regimes. The unwelcome reader is always there whether you've seen him in print yet or not, and thinking about how and why he misreads you will help you develop a more engaged sense of audience and purpose. If you succeed, the unwelcome reader himself, not you, may be the one who suddenly realizes he's standing in the street with his pants down.

THE STRANGERS

on the night my internationally adopted son arrived

After we picked you up at the Omaha airport,
we clamped you into a new car seat
and listened to you yowl beneath
the streetlights of Nebraska.

Our hotel suite was plump with toys,
ready, we hoped, to soothe you into America.
But for a solid hour you watched the door,
shrieking, *Amma*, the Korean word for mother.

Once or twice you glanced back at us
and, in this netherworld where a door home
had slammed shut forever, your terrified eyes
paced between the past and the future.

Amma, you screamed. *Amma!*
But your foster mother back in Seoul never appeared.

Your new mother and I lay on the bed,
cooing your birth name, *Min-gyu*,
until, at last, you collapsed into our arms.
In time, even terror must yield to sleep.

Stacia M. Fleegal

Find the Girl in Echo Park & Take Her Apart: A Review of Three Small Press Titles Seeking the Female

There are pieces of her everywhere.

Fortunately for us, there are writers skilled in search and excavation, writers so careful with language that even without a chronological narrative, their stories still ring utterly true. Three of those writers are Molly Gaudry, Christine Hamm, and Lightsey Darst.

Three modern literary works, written by three formidably talented women, published by three quality small presses. All three emphasize language over genre, feature both urban and natural settings, and return to origin as the "true north" of their respective narrators. All three posit the female as lost or broken, but healing, sojourning, examining other females, all wide eyes and courageous bruises. All three utilize fairy tale imagery, earthy vignettes, and fragmented or disjointed phrasing that enviably cohere in mood and tone.

Molly Gaudry's debut novella *We Take Me Apart* (Mud Luscious Press) begins with a mother's bedtime fable of a woman being dismembered and cooked in her own stew; and just that swiftly, the metaphor of a woman in pieces takes off. By page 24, the daughter-narrator herself is being consumed, "brought to winter lips / in warm moist mouths dissolve." Gaudry navigates the early mother-daughter relationship, the give-and-take nature of teaching a girl to be a girl, and at what cost. Of a very pregnant elephant, the narrator observes that "everyone...loved her all the more for her fatness." Of her mother, the narrator poignantly states, "Happiness was her hoped for ever after // then I came along & in this version happiness / was her hoped for ever after for me." Class is implicated (an obsession with cleanliness and food, of which there is little), but gender is at the forefront: Gaudry's book tirelessly examines body image and body parts, fashion, cooking/eating, intimacy, and ritual with lyrical deftness and an admirable neurosis for choosing the perfect word every time. A Molly Gaudry word is so precise, it feels like a sentence.

But there is no end punctuation, and often more fragments than sentences. Among writers with a reverence for "forming" subject matter, here is one who is unafraid to make a bold statement about the nature of the feminine as being parts of an unknown or unfixed sum, rather than the opposite. The novella spans nearly the entire life of the female speaker who refers often (in retrospect) to her "stitching years"— those she spent self-sustained via an initially happy partnership and her talent for creating dresses, in construction of an identity, in pursuit of a way to put all the pieces together. Gaudry memorably employs fairy tales and myths, always introducing them with "In a different version..." In Gaudry's versions, though, there is no soapbox. The images of domesticity and their inferences—that women are born to be taken from, taken apart—do not commit to either victimhood or subversion. Does Gaudry write of womanhood in fragments because women are broken, or is she writing in defiance of a global, concrete definition of The Female? In *We Take Me Apart*, Gaudry shows great restraint in merely raising—rather than presumptuously resolving— questions we as readers want to try to answer, to join the narrator and her mother on p. 92 as they attempt to save the world: "their hurt was once the fragile middle of a pearl / but our arrival is the purple shine of the pearl."

If Gaudry's book is the life of a girl, Christine Hamm's third collection of poetry, *Echo Park* (BlazeVOX [books]), is more concerned with where a girl goes when she heads off on her own, into "the woods" (if a girl screams in the woods/park and no one hears her, is there even an echo?). The third poem in the collection features an adolescent female's suicide attempt, the first instance of "unravel[ing]." Where Gaudry draws parallels from myth and fairy tales, Hamm overtly titles her poems "How to Make a Person" and "The Selling of the Parts," the latter of which is incidentally sandwiched between two fragment/list poems. At p. 31, we come to the first poem in prose—featuring line and stanza break notations, but with the same clipped rhythm of the 30 preceding pages of shorter lines. A physical attempt to "put the pieces together"? Knife and scissor imagery in the poem "Year 12," the threat of being eaten by an unknown predator in "Dorothy in the Dark Woods," "The Grass Eater" and its industrial image of the female being "milked" of all she has to offer—Gaudry's preoccupations are Hamm's as well, but *Echo Park* names more names. Tristessa, Susan, Lucia, Joan of Arc (a heroine working at The Gap, how sadly modern!), three poems for Dorothy of Kansas, and a character sketch of one of the 1911 Triangle Shirtwaist Fire victims, Hamm clearly wants female voices to be heard. When describing a sexual encounter in "Landscape at Night with Bed and Fire," she tells us that "The room shudders, a bedful of red snakes; / the room stills, a bedful of drowned plates" (p. 37). With such fresh and gorgeous lines, I'd argue Hamm's is one of those must-hear voices.

But what of the rest of the voiceless, victims in the stories we're told as little girls about what can happen to us? Lightsey Darst's *Find the Girl* (Coffee House Press) is a cautionary tale of what happens "in the woods," one warning after another about avoiding a seemingly unavoidable fate. Darst's poems return over and over to the spring greenness of female adolescence. Our narrator is at turns historian, lead detective, medical examiner, storm crow... And so many girls to find! Debutantes and prom queens who only "climb" in their dreams, teenagers trying out independence with brutal consequences, Darst races to "Find the girl in time," before she "wind[s] up in the newspaper with her feet // photographed bare sticking out from under / a rhododendron bush" (p. 20).

Alas, they cannot all be saved ("I found the girl. Don't hear glory. I like to dig." p. 31). These are not victories; girls will still be lost, or only found in parts. Darst, then, turns to critical analysis—"What do they want of you?" she asks of Helen of Troy (p. 22)—and definitions. She lets other voices, some male and some female, tell us that, "Not everyone will mistake [a girl] for a fairy princess" (p. 15), and "A girl is a woman / is a rack to be hung with gashed sky..." (p. 41), "you can dress her, sooth her, / make her feel fear" (p. 40), and "A saint is a girl who dies young / before you know otherwise" (p. 63). In "[*1888, London*]," Darst references Jack the Ripper: "The news is, ladies are being murdered / by a man who's searching for (kissed me / on the stairs) something he lost / inside them" (p. 14). Girls lost and broken haunt these pages in a mosaic of new bras and old warnings, dresses and charm bracelets, image and fable. (Darst, like Gaudry and Hamm, conjures myth and legend; she mentions crones, maidens, witches, goddesses, and rituals, all of which lend a mystical overtone, as if asking the questions or even attempting to "find the girl" is an alchemy of sorts.) That the lyric difficulty of these poems makes for a sometimes challenging read is a strong testimony to their authenticity and the authority of the poet. It is not unbelievable to us that every girl mentioned in this book could die of femaleness.

Katie Ford's blurb intuits that Darst is "dutiful to the women and girls long lost from poetry," adding that "...the elegy of our time cannot resurrect the dead into an idealized heaven but must, instead, lay bare those words and deeds that batter a life until it is perceived 'as a sewer,' a plaything, a pageantry or a curse..." Three books by three women, all fairly recently published (Gaudry's is in its third printing), all concerning the female in parts, all in light of the now-infamous VIDA count, the continued decimation of women's reproductive and civil rights, and the fact that women still earn a quarter less an hour than their male counterparts with the same job titles: is this the political made personal?

It isn't that the authors are overtly defining what it means to be female. In fact, they are operating under the assumption that you and I know, as they do, that no such definition exists, that only capitalism needs one. Still, women live in a world where we must, if we venture out alone, look over our shoulders. Fact. Finishing these books is like coming to that moment in a post-apocalyptic movie when all the precursors and catalysts that had seemed so far-fetched snap with eerie relevance—*this IS the world we live in!* Gaudry, Hamm, and Darst are doing the age old work of women writers: insisting they have a story worth telling and crafting irresistible and innovative ways to make us listen.

Matt Ryan

AN ALIEN SPEAKS

Humans: My telescope is better than yours. I purchased some of those telescope enlargement pills that I found advertised in your email account. Now my partner is crazy about the size of my telescope. Humans: I sometimes hack your email account because your position on privacy issues amuses me. Here is a side note: my family has been sick. We've had a little case of gonorrhea that we keep passing around to one another. I have germs inside of me—one named Fritz, the other Wolfgang—that are dying. Don't worry: they will be nursed back to good health, and when this happens, my telescope doubles as a gonorrhea launcher and I will send Fritz and Wolfgang your way. We have sex up here and it's time you deal with it. Humans: I'm unmoved that you think it's gross. When you talk out of your ass, I can follow along because I am buttlingual. I understand the secrets of the anus. There is no secret password that can conceal this truth forever.

Emily Oliver

Emily Oliver of the Knox Writers' House answers some questions

The brainchild of three Knox College English majors, Knox Writer's House is a virtual house found online at knoxwritershouse.com. It's a Winchester-Mansion-like, always-being-built abode lavish with "poems, stories, essays, and interviews of nearly one hundred writers from Chicago to Madison to the Twin Cities to Kalamazoo to St. Louis to Kansas City . . . going south to New Orleans, east to Atlanta, further east to New York, New Haven, Providence." When you go to the KWH homepage, you find a Google map of the United States—literally, a "map of voices"—with interactive green Google teardrops marking the places where each of the recorded writers live, a click being the only distance between you and a wealth of voices, a wealth of words. This interview is with one of the founders.

Matt Mauch: *If you had to capture the essence of your venture in a promotional short form like a book blurb—you know, three to five lightning-rod sentences—what would you say (and hint: keep these for your press releases)?*

EO: The Knox Writers' House is audio map of American Poetry, Essays and Stories. It aspires to become a map of North, South and Central American Contemporary Literature. We ask writers to read some of their own work, a 'best-loved' poem or piece of prose by someone else and then interview them briefly about where they live. The Knox Writers' House is a project about kinship, geographic but also literary kinship, about the communal passing of awe through words.

MM: *Back in the print era, I and some business partners (which may or may not be hard to come to terms with, but is what you all are) started up a Village Voice-esque publication in a medium-*

sized Midwestern city. One of the greatest parts of the start-up was researching all that was out there—driving from city to city to collect each city's weekly so we didn't reinvent the wheel (unless doing so was appropriate). What, for you, has been greatest part of The Knox Writers' House start-up?

EO: In terms of research, I did this amazing (because of the instructor and work read) independent study on Midwestern writers before the very first summer of recording. This all started because I emailed ten of the people I read for that class and they all got back to me – starting with the fiction writer Peter Orner, who wasn't even living in the Midwest at the time. They not only agreed to be recorded for what I was thinking would be a podcast series, that I called (in my head) Knox Writers' House: A Map of Voices from the American Midwest or Stories and Poems in the Midwest or something like that. The most beautiful thing about this project was how, as soon as Bryce, Sammie, and I got in the car, it turned into something different. Something about the road through the hills into Minnesota that first summer, the expanse of the Midwestern sky, the type of friendship and coconspirator camaraderie we had between us changed the scope and concerns of the Knox Writers' House recording project.

MM: *What's in the basement of The Knox Writers' House? What, that is, are the things, people, experiences, etc., that inspired you to build it, and remain, albeit underground, as your foundation?*

EO: I've always loved hearing written work read out loud. I grew up with terrible eyesight and a lot of learning difficulties so maybe that has something to do with it. But when I transferred to Knox College, I did a small-scale recording project by the same name, just recording Knox College Creative Writing Dept faculty and students. Honestly, this was in some part a way for me to make friends and get to know the department and it worked. I used a handheld digital voice record that I stole from the AV department. The sound quality of those recordings are completely awful but it did teach me how to design and carry out a project like this. Then, the next fall I studied abroad in Buenos Aires, Argentina, and the first day I got there met a poet (who wrote in Spanish obviously) who gave me a copy of her book. I went to BA not knowing very much Spanish and it took me a MONTH to get through her book looking up every other word. I ended up doing a project recording her and about 12 other writers in her circle, either recommended directly by her or by someone she recommended. It was crazy because I had been living there for months but it wasn't until I asked in those interviews *how do you make a life as a writer in Buenos Aires?* that I started to understand the character of that city. I came back and realized I was making my life in the Midwest, where I had never been before I was 20, with ignorance or even dismissal of its character. I had a gotten a fellowship and needed to write up a proposal so that's how it all got started. Then I did that wonderful Midwestern Writers class with Poet / Knox College Professor Monica Berlin, who in many ways is herself the foundation of the Knox Writers' House. She has at least occasionally told us where to pour the cement.

MM: *You came over to my house after a night at Pocket Lab, followed by cocktails at the 331, on a sultry-ass summer day when we may have actually broken a dew-point record in these Cities Twin, recording me and another TC poet and in the process christening my version of that Minnesota staple, the basement bar. I only have the one story, but you've got to have hundreds. What have been some of the cooler or crazier things you've done that you'll one day wax nostalgic about?*

EO: There are so many. I could write pages and page, Matt. It is crazy because so many good ones happen in the Twin Cities. For me, that is the place we this project was really born that first summer. I love the story of how we asked Lon Otto to read a 'best-loved' without giving him any warning beforehand because we had just decided to do it on the drive up to the Twin Cities. He bounded up the narrow stairs of his beautiful Victorian (or whatever) and got his copy of William Faulkner's *As I Lay Dying* and read us the whole Addie chapter without so much as clearing his throat. He couldn't have practiced because we had asked him right there, but the only thing I edited out of that sound file is all of us at his kitchen table, sighing.

Also, and again, in the Cities, we recorded Paula Cisewski, John Colburn and Sarah Fox at Paula and her husband, the artist, Jack Walsh's house. We were at their kitchen table for hours. I so admired the way Paula and Jack lived their lives, the way they make art at the center of their lives. That night in their kitchen held this particular magic. Bryce, his farm boy smile, asking this earnest questions about who poetry is for and Sammie speaking his easy way that makes everyone instantly endeared to him. It almost felt religious. Afterward, we sat in the car on the street for twenty minutes with my laptop in my lap just listening over again to the poems we'd just recorded. Bryce read a crumpled, folded print-out John Colburn's "First Impressions" – which is very much a poem about being the age we were (and are) and the heartache of that – with this big eyed awe. And then we had this furious drive back to where we were staying in St. Paul that night, Sammie driving reckless, all of us speaking this furious talk about art and our lives and what we could make. I don't know another way to say it – those boys were my journeymen.

MM: *So, softball question time. There are poetry sites out there, like the $100 million Poetry Foundation site. Poets, publishers, and the poetically inclined have 'em linked and bookmarked. As the new kid on the block, what doth distinguish The Knox Writers' House (I call this a softball question because I think there are oodles of things that make you you)?*

EO: We are making an archive of people who self identify as writers. We are not making editorial choices about one school, one type, one poem over another we. We go to a city and document people who write there. It has to do with how we find people too. Sometimes, we've read people and email them but more often than not we ask for recommendations from writers we've recorded or read previously about the next location we are heading to. We email those people and record the ones that get back to us. We record everyone in person, the vast majority of them at their homes. Our ambition is different than other institutions. We have recorded poet laureates, Pulitzer Prize winners and *New York Times* best sellers that were really amazing but we've also recorded unpublished backwoods geniuses that totally knocked us on our ass. We have always run on a shoe string budget, begging small grants here/there just for gas, slept on the floor of friends or friends of friends and sometimes strangers, and we record as many people of a place as we can in the time we are there. We are kind of an underground operation and we are interested in underground art. Also, because we were students and didn't really know who was famous (even poetry famous) and who wasn't, especially at the start of this, some of our charming ignorance has worn off in the process. We just emailed people whose work we'd admired and people those people recommended.

MM: *If the GOD OF THINGS HENCE came to you in the form of a boxelder bug and asked, job-interview style, "Where do yourself five years from now?" what would say about The Knox Writers' House? Will you still be recording poets? Will you have expanded? Will you become a nonprofit? Will you expand services? How will the world have changed because of you? Tell us what you see in your crystal ball.*

EO: I'm kind of a restless girls so I am always making plans. First of all, with Knox Writers House, we are currently in the process of starting up a Knox Writers' House Contributors' Pick of the Week where we ask a writer we recorded to choose a poem or story they like from the site. We are going to post them weekly on KWH facebook page and our newly created Twitter and podcast blog. The weekly Pick is how we are going to build our podcast in iTunes. The writer picking has the option of writing a little paragraph about their choice, writing something in conversation with or in the style of their choice or they can just send the link out naked. It would be like:

Blah Blah by Blah Blah
Chosen by Matt Mauch in the Twin Cities.
link to your page

(optional paragraph or thing)

So far we have a commitment from Philip Levine to do one
for like six weeks from now to herald in the NY writers I
recorded over December when we get them up on the site
but that's it. If you come across something, I love for you to
pick at some point. You are like the 6th person I've told this
idea to so if you have any suggestions let me know. Anyway,
I think the optional paragraph is a kind of cool way to keep
the conversation going among the writers we recorded. I love
recording writers. It is my absolute favorite thing to do. I
hope to keep doing it. I hope we get more money to go more
places to do more with the site. I hope to keep recording.

MM: *What about The Knox House lifeblood, i.e., you as an
individual person—what are you up to? Striving for? Thinking
about? Making? Selling? Studying? Writing? Doing? Give us a
glimpse into the reality show you call your life.*

EO: Honestly, I hope to be able to keep doing this above
anything else. I love recording. I love our site. I love this
project. But I did just apply to some poetry MFA grad
programs and I want to someday get a Fullbright to record
more Spanish and or Portuguese language writers. I need to
sharpen my language skills a little. Eventually, I want to work
on 'audio translations' in part inspired by the recording of the
Twin Cities own Kristin Naca's reading Pablo Neruda's "Una"
and the translation "One" as her best-loved and partly by
Robert Hass reading us his translation of a Frida Kahlo poem.
I also just loved Latin American Literature.

I am really interested in using KWH recorded audio to do
sound instillations and celebrations with other types of
artists. I'm currently involved in an instillation piece with
a sculptor at Knox this winter who has made a translucent

dome from space blankets that he inflates with an air conditioning unit. Three people at time lay down on their back in the dome while an audio poem is played. I am also involved in a collaboration called *On Galesburg*. For this, an audience will sit facing a wall of the 306 Simmons Poetry Space in Galesburg, IL, while photography from local photo expeditions is project beside the text of poems by local poets and the audio of these poems is simultaneously played. It is the ambition of these projects to explore not merely what words do on the daily level but how we experience them. I think these are ways poetry can function in communities to bring us closer to ourselves. That sounds pretentious. I don't mean it pretentious. It is super fucking silly. Space blanket dome...

MM: *And you're moving to the Twin Cities when?*

EO: I'd love to live in the Twin Cities. I'll let you know if the MFA program at UM Twin Cities is down and you let me know if you hear of any employment.

Open-Mic Poems

The innaugural and second annual Great Twin Cities Poetry Reads concluded with an 10-or-so-minute open mic. The names of audience members who had placed them, during the 10-or-so-minute intermission, into the ceremonial PRB beer stein were drawn out and the poets who'd come with poems to read came one by one to the stage. And they read their poems, some of which were included in **Poetry City, USA, Vol. 1**, and some of which are included here.*

When the Great Twin Cities Poetry Read morphed into the Great Twin Cities Poetry Read + Road Show in the summer of 2011**, bimonthly readings at Maeve's Cafe on NE Mpls's famous Poetry Row—called The Maeve's Sessions— become the new standing home of the GTCPR + RS open mic. The poems in the six pages that follow were read there.

* Sponsored by the Pocket Lab Reading Series
** Many thanks to Sean Hill, who in conversations arranging a Road Show event in Bemidji came up with the "Road Show" monicker

Caitlin Bailey

WILD BOAT

Your presence demanded my tongue and so I made my body
an armory, took to lying under the floorboards. My heart became
a wild boat, in a storm in a haze in an hour, and its anchor grew
beneath me. I imagined it taking root on the seabed, twined
around a blind fish or scarred with kelp. It became harder
to leave the room and I stared at the chipped tile to pass the time.
Your coat was strung on a line in the bathroom and so I couldn't
ignore it. It remained true that you died in a bed in Poland
and that I hid from your death. It was worse than all the other facts.

NOTES ON FLYING

First, the violins, and then
the impossible girl,
arms splayed wide,
glides like the first human ever.

The blade of her body sings,
and, somewhere,
a well played piano.

Her fingers seem to feather
and lightly touch the sky.

She flies!

Enters, a higher register.

Penultimately, it's the tympanis,
as she calmly performs a miracle
and nimbly turns into a cloud,
and, at last, crash cymbals
when you think you just might know
this isn't skydiving!

She's never coming home.

Scott Vetsch

CHRISTMAS LETTER

Dear Nola,

Happy to hear you caught another wedding bouquet,
hope the bedbugs don't mess up your game.
Yes, it's true, I'm living the fairy tale,
dating the Whore of Babylon, dumb with pleasure.
Overhead black helicopters blowback a conspiracy of
Ex-Nazis, proto-Stalinists, Mormon revisionists,
UFO's, and capitalists drunk on Jesus.

No wolf in the woods, no mermaid on a rock.
I'm a field of wheat,
sown, irrigated, and cultivated,
a John Barleycorn affair, obscenely ripe head,
a honeybee collecting pollen,
a rattlesnake producing venom,
a blizzard of mayflies on an August night.

I'm milked:
venom or cream, viper and cow,
harvested, husbanded, pruned and picked,
an empty nursing home bed,
a gold-tooth, and two titanium screws.

In this fairy tale we embrace a world numbed
by god and football, extol its amazing Asian
fireless flame technology handcrafted by the Amish,
revere a freezer-full of frozen pheasant breasts,
bucket-lunch for Cassandra dozing in her hope-chest,
humming along to some brass-age lullaby,
heartfelt ode to Licorice Dick's Road-House Gravy.

We crossed the river,
power-chord couple nursing a busted whammy bar,
seeking sustain, navigating the trans-suburban highway,
guided by stars, crippled by doubt.

MANONAM

Eventually, once eternity
begins its kind retreat
and we are meant to live
all of this again

(but backwards)

You'll be the kind of woman
(when I am a man)
that I will meet
and love
in college

h.c. wiederholt

THE BAKER

I wish I had three arms
said the baker
sifting flour.

BLONDE *adj.*

One of the few adjectives in English to retain
separate masculine and feminine genders. *Sandy*.
Have waterfall halos in the sunshine on the campus mall,
have more fun at the party, the kegger, wherever. *Ash*. Hitchcock
said they make the best victims
"like virgin snow that shows up the bloody footprints." *Golden*.
As noun, preceded by one of the following adjectives:
dumb, suicide, dizzy. *Peroxide*. Marker of youth. *Strawberry*.
In fairy tales, is trapped, caged, comatose,
in danger of being eaten: Goldilocks
almost eaten by a cross-dressing wolf, Sleeping Beauty
comatosed by a jealous brunette, Rapunzel
locked in a tower, Cinderella scrubbing in rags, Gretel
tricked by a cannibalistic witch. *Platinum*. Studies show
contemporary women who dye their hair blonde
feel more attractive and sexually confident
and are more likely to question authority. *Dirty*.
The only minority for which—despite
harassment, stereotypes, sexism, and open ridicule—
women take drastic measures
in order to be included. *Natural*.

A note on The Maeve's Sessions

The Maeve's Sessions are held on the first Thursday of every other month, alternating months with the Pocket Lab Reading Series. Maeve's Sessions are held at Maeve's Cafe* and Pocket Lab Reading Series events are held at the Rogue Buddha Gallery. Add to the mix the Bosso Poetry Company readings at Dusty's Bar and Center for Visionary Poetics readings at Spot Art Gallery, and you have something we like to call NE Mpls's famous Poetry Row**.

Maeve's Sessions readings feature three or so readers, followed by a 10-or-so-minute open mic. Open mic readers put their names in the ceremonial PBR beet stein, from which they are randomly pulled until the 10-or-minutes expires. Featured Maeve's readers donate a copy of their published books, if they have one or several, to Maeve's Poetry Shelf. Patrons have the option of feeding their hearts, minds, and souls in addition to their bellies. Featured readers also sign a copy of a poem they read with their photo on it. These poems are hung along Maeve's Poet's Wall/Hall of Fame, right next the bathrooms.

* Thanks to proprietor Mary Cassidy. Do stop in and say "hi." Tell her the muse sent you.

** "Lest the city list to the Eat Street side," he said.

Cass Dalglish

On Moral Fiction

K.'s a guy who knows about fiction and he says all
you need is a character and an existential question.
So you look around, and you see a girl – thin face,
bony nose – half sitting, half reclining on a blue-green
couch in the off-white library of a garden level
apartment, sipping a virgin Margarita and thinking
about the good old days when books told her what
was right and what was wrong.

She says her name is Donna Q., and she has a wolf
hybrid who's really sweet if he's not angry, and when
he spots you, it's obvious he hasn't made up his mind.
"You coming or going?" she asks and you know you
mean to hang around, maybe take her off somewhere
you feel she's compelled to go. You hear a growl,
part dog, part wolf. She says the animal's name is
Cusp and half the time he wants to run in the woods.

"Is that where you plan to take me?" she asks, 'cause
she's thinking maybe she won't go. Maybe she'd
rather follow the wind across the open plains.
You tell her that's her question, and it's a worthy one,
and you're going to stay with her 'til she answers it,
no matter how long it takes because her story might
not be a short one. And next thing you know she's
wearing a yellow-orange sheath and a pair of patent
leather shoes. "The soles are Nike," she says and she's
outta there. Cusp is gone too.

"Stop there," K. says, "that's the end." But you can't
believe it. So you tell the guy, "I don't believe it,"
and K. tells you to embrace your doubt! And you ask
him what kind of wise crack that is, and he says it's
the wisdom of uncertainty. He says, "Check it out
with Cervantes." He says it's the only responsibility
any fiction writer has.

* apologies to Gardner, thanks to Kundera

RARA AVIS 1913

in memoriam Charles W. Scrutchin, attorney at law

Flash of yellow
against all that white,
a daffodil against
the snow, white as
your parrot in its cage
kept in the house
from the interminable
snows of a Bemidji
winter waiting for summer
when townsfolk strolling
along the sidewalk
in front of your house
start at its thunderbolt squawk—
lightning against cerulean—
as expected here as you, black
like the wrought iron bars
of the cage containing
the parrot, white as
your wife or as a barrister's
powdered wig—black against
white like your fingers caressing
the pages of law books,
grasping them, needful
as that parrot's squawking,
finally on the porch in its cage,
a tuft of feathers atop its head
raised revealing
the tint of daffodils.

Tim Nolan

My Reading

I am a promiscuous reader. I read a lot, but I have few loyalties. I think of the collection of books I am reading at any given time as the reverse image of me at that given time. If someone (not me) could assemble a list of all I have read, it might say everything (or nothing) about me.

For awhile a few years ago, I read everything I could about Americans in Paris in the 1920's—Fitzgerald, Hemingway, Gertrude Stein, Man Ray, Man Ray's very talented and beautiful lover, Lee Miller, who took some of the great photographs of postwar Europe.

One book led to another, one biography to another, until I had assembled what seemed to be a whole story called *Paris in the 1920's* or *Americans Abroad*. I would read pairs of dueling memoirs (Morley Callaghan's *That Summer in Paris* vs. Hemingway's *A Moveable Feast*). I read the *Selected Letters of Ernest Hemingway* vs. The *Selected Letters of John Dos Passos*. My interest in all the characters was endless and spiraling down, that is, one book led me to another, making me think I could finally figure things out. Fitzgerald's view of Gerald Murphy vs. Murphy's view of Fitzgerald.

The only benefit of all of this work is that I may know as much as Woody Allen about the characters in his movie *Midnight in Paris*. That's the only benefit I can think of from all my reading about Paris in the 1920's.

Except earlier this year, when our 17-year-old son announced one afternoon that he had just finished *The Great Gatsby*, and thought it was *pretty amazing*, I wrote a poem that drew on some of that otherwise useless knowledge. I was struck and pleased that afternoon by Frank's enthusiasm about the last few pages of *The Great Gatsby* which are about as good as anything that has been written.

The Great Gatsby

Our son Frank just finished
reading *The Great Gatsby*

we should have a party
And he is telling me
all about Irving Thalberg
and *The Last Tycoon*—so

I take off the shelf
a dusty copy of *Tender Is
the Night* and hand it

To him and he removes the dust
and shakes his hands
of the dust—isn't this the way

It works?—And we talk
about those last pages of
The Great Gatsby and Wisconsin

And coming home at Christmas—
and he says—*It was mostly
perfect*—which I have said—

I think I said that
recently—I said that
to somebody vehemently—

And I can tell Frank
feels the same way—that he
will say this over again

To anyone who will listen—
It's hard to explain our
parochial ways—the closeness

Of our parish—the *thereness*
of this sidewalk—how love
(what else is it?)—seeps through

The sliver of the fourteenth
dimension to right now—the snow
in the night from a moving window

As a poet, my reading can only be described as *slapdash*. Since I don't understand in advance what I may need to know for a poem, or what I may stumble upon as I'm doodling, I look upon my reading as *cutting a wide swath through the dense woods*. I tend to not read fiction much, because I'm not really looking for character and plot—rather, I'm looking for some historical coincidence, or some image that I think may be true. I find I cannot make a sustained commitment to plot and character if that commitment lasts more than a few pages. Poems with a strong narrative element are more satisfying (and efficient) for me than novels or even short stories.

I read lots of poems as they appear in my email or on Facebook. They may be from the 19th century or from yesterday, good or not so good. I read so many poems that I tend to just glance at the first few lines, before deciding whether to commit myself to the whole poem. Lord Byron, when he appears out of the past, does not fare so well. But John Milton still looks good, and anything by Shakespeare that lands on my computer screen makes me pause.

I read many books of contemporary poetry, but again, I do so in a jumpy and erratic way. I will read the first poem and the last poem in a book, and then try to imagine what might happen in between. Rarely do I read a book of poems from beginning to end, unless the book is by Louise Glück, Jack Gilbert, W.S. Merwin, some others, and then I feel I must honor their mastery.

Non-fiction of all kinds is my main meat. History, biography, letters, memoir. I love when a subject, long dead, begins to occupy my thoughts and dreams, as if I knew them, as if we had lunch the other day. I'm drawn to anything about Anton Chekhov, William Carlos Williams, Marilyn Monroe, any of the Kennedys, Lee Harvey Oswald, James Laughlin, F. Scott Fitzgerald, Zelda Fitzgerald, and anything about Abraham Lincoln, as well as Walt Whitman, Emily Dickinson, Jesus, and the Buddha.

I try, mostly without success, to read about particle physics, cosmology, the human genome, the Higgs Boson, but I come to those books so lacking in basic understanding that I tend to quickly abandon the effort.

Instead, I find myself reading *Going Rogue* by Sarah Palin, a memoir by Joey Bishop, a biography of Mickey Mantle. For awhile, I was very interested in Hollywood sex scandals of the early part of the 20th century. *Hollywood Babylon* by Kenneth Anger is perhaps the very best trashy and absolutely entertaining books I have ever read. After I read it, I felt thoroughly corrupted, as if I had been allowed into the real world of passion, stupidity and complete vice. As I read *Hollywood Babylon*, I somehow regretted that each scandalous story, each word, brought me closer to the end. Fortunately, there is a *Hollywood Babylon II*, if you are interested.

I generally avoid kings, queens, royalty, as well as popes, philosophy, and self-help books. I've never read a book in the *How To for Dummies* series. I like cookbooks, but that's not reading in my mind. It's just following directions.

When I'm feeling scholarly, I like to read about Shakespeare. I'm fascinated by the mystery and wonder of his life—the speculation about his *missing years*—where was he? Was he a Roman Catholic? What caused him to leave his wife and children in Stratford to set out for the big city to make his way? Shakespeare's journey is like a variation on the departure of Siddhartha Gautama (the Buddha) from his palace out into the real world of suffering and death.

I like to read about ghosts, tales from *the other side*, the historical Jesus, astrophysics, string theory, the Bermuda Triangle, Walt Whitman's years in Washington, D.C., during the Civil War, the East Village in New York City in the 1970's, musical comedies of the 1950's, D-Day.

None of this does me any measurable good, but I don't think it does me any harm.

Sometimes, my reading comes into my poetry. Years ago, I was interested in the space program. Of course I read Tom Wolfe's *The Right Stuff*. I read some books by and about the Apollo astronauts.

One afternoon, out in the front yard, I quickly wrote a poem called "Old Astronauts." I knew Buzz Aldrin had difficult times with alcohol and divorce after his trip to the Moon in 1969. I remember reading somewhere that he had fallen in the bathroom. I also read about a former astronaut, James Irwin, who became a born-again Christian after going to the Moon, and led several trips to Mount Ararat to try to find Noah's Ark. These details, all from my random reading, made their way into my poem.

Old Astronauts

When they get together now—
they nod to one another—

don't talk about the pitch-
black of airless space—

don't want to remember
the dust of the Moon

in the treads of their boots—
They fall in bathrooms—

just like everyone else—
but from a greater height—

and before their heads
hit the tiled floor—

they float for awhile—
weightless—seeming to dance

at the end of a cord—
One of them found

Noah's Ark—or is just
about to—mostly—they

remain dead silent—
Whatever they saw and felt—

lost for generations—it's that

they were led to believe

they really could escape—
the pull—of the molten core—

Today, as I look at the contents of my Barnes & Noble Nook Color, I see that I have downloaded the following books in the last few days:

Not Afraid of Life: A Memoir
by Bristol Palin

The Story of Charlotte's Web: E.B. White's Eccentric Life in Nature and the Birth of an American Classic
by Michael Sims

Sleeping with the Enemy: Coco Chanel's Secret War
by Hal Vaughan

Ordinary Geniuses: Max Delbruck, George Gamow, and the Origins of Genomics and Big Bang Cosmology
by Gino Segre

Neil Young: Long May You Run: The Illustrated History
by Daniel Durchholz and Gary Graff

Cod: A Biography of the Fish that Changed the World
by Mark Kurlansky

My Spiritual Life
by The Dalai Lama

Never Letting Go: Heal Grief with Help from the Other Side
by Mark Anthony

Ten Letters: The Stories Americans Tell Their President
by Eli Saslow

A War Like No Other: How the Athenians and Spartans
Fought the Peloponnesian War
  by Victor Davis Hanson

The Flooded Earth: Our Future in a World without Ice Caps
by Peter D. Ward

I may end up reading only the book by Bristol Palin. Maybe one or two others. The information I take in may serve no purpose ever. I will probably look at the pictures in the Neil Young book, at the very least.

I've learned that when you download books from the library, you only get them for 21 days. I've also learned that you never have to return the book. At the end of the 21st day, the book just disappears from the Nook Color. Similarly, the book disappears from my mind—until I need it. Then—I vaguely remember—*there was something I once read.*

Lynette Reini-Grandell

THE THOROUGHBRED'S BLACK KNEES

I open the gate
and shock to the touch of her swan-black neck.
It dips, it nuzzles, it forages.
She eyes me,
then gazes back to the animal world.

Change jangles in my pocket like broken glass.
This horse is all compulsive locomotion,
she pulls me under her wing,
in her I trust the lemon sunlight,
the invisible grass,
the summoning song.

It is the most natural thing in the world to depend on each other,
we work together,
we put away the dead,
we burn with forward movement.

This dark horse whispers art is not death,
it is temporary, miraculous escape from death,
a cat in the night under a leafless rose bush
a calm, seated figure
floating above the ripples of an otherwise still pond:
me,
knocked down,
breathless,
turning to the sight of a thousand-pound horse
rushing the gate
and leaping over my head.

Her black, knobby knees contract and pump in my face like fists
named danger and fear,
each trembling hair vast yet finite,
then her hooves are past me,
drumming unexpected survival.

Kathryn Kysar

Perfect Pictures: A review of Jim Moore's *Invisible Strings* (Graywolf Press)

I came to Jim Moore's work late. I knew he was revered in the Twin Cities as a founding member of the Loft Literary Center, a beloved graduate professor in the MALS and MFA programs at Hamline, but I had read little of his work. When I finally opened up *Invisible Strings*, I was delighted to find imagistic poems, a la Williams, Pound, and H.D. Imagism was born as a literary response to the photograph, and Moore uses the poem as a camera to create a deep, meaningful sequence of pictures in this poignant book.

The collection is filled with Moore's wry observations, poems that distilled a moment, often bittersweet, to a few spare lines. In "Sleeping with Mona Lisa," the speaker observes "The young woman on the train/uses as a bookmark/a postcard of the Mona Lisa./She sleeps, while in the distant field/at the edge of the painting/just poking up through her book/I see the light da Vinci loved/the blue light of ambulances at night/when they pulse out their warnings."

Pulsing their warnings at the edges and sometimes the center of the poems, death, and its companion, age, create a lens of regret. From "Saturday":

I was in the middle of reading
  Yet another poem about death
when I looked up. A man was standing there
  hand open, silently hoping
I might give.

  He stared straight at me,
The brown skin of his palm like a blind eye
  looking out into nothing.
I shook my head no
  And went back to my book, death

returning to death.

In other poems, the speaker ponders age as he turns sixty, feeling the weight of the being the oldest generation now that his mother has passed away.

The sections of the book are organized by place: Only Everywhere, Spoleto, St. Paul, Disappearing in America, St. Paul, Spoleto. Just as many poems' tensions come from juxtaposing incongruent images, the book's tension comes from juxtaposing disparate places as it moves between the United States and Italy. In the poem "After Dinner," the two worlds come together. The American speaker does not know Italian but sits, listening with greater understanding as the evening goes on: "For many years, unable to speak the language/I have sat silently at tables with Italians./ Tonight, too. But this time I don't mind./Joy enters the voices. Then sadness./We sit in moonlight, drinking wine/ until I understand every last word." The reoccurring tensions between sadness and joy, regret and happiness, silence and talking, occur in many poems, often synthesizing into a small twinkle of understanding at the end of the poem, as in "After Dinner." "Not Taking It Personally" labels its three sections 1(Thesis) 2 (Antithesis) 3(Synthesis), cueing the reader into the key organizational pattern not only for this poem but the book.

Moore makes his titles work. In the small poems, the titles often set the scene, as in "Waiting to Take Off": "I try not to listen to the direction/to the emergency exits,/how close they are,/ how very well lit." Learning from fellow Minnesota poet Robert Bly's early 1960s poem titles that simply stated the place and time, Moore at times takes this concept farther, describing the key event and then examining the aftermath, such as in "Blood in our Headlights, Car Wrecked, the Boar Dead." He is not afraid to play with his reader's expectations: a series of poems from a Spoleto section are titled for sequential week days, then "Saturday" ironically discusses an event from the day before.

The poems are almost uniform in shape and structure, a small line set above the others as a title (and sometimes it is the title), looking slightly fragmented but highly consistent as to not distract the reader from the book's content and voice. The poems are perfectly punctuated, and Moore is not afraid of internal periods and sentence fragments. These small poems need to be read slowly, carefully, and the line breaks and internal full stops slow the reader down.

Each word in these imagistic poems has been carefully contemplated, but not at the sacrifice of voice. The poet often converses with himself (and the reader), commenting on his own poems, with an "Of course," or "Pathetic, I know" when discussing his own vices. The poems often end on a keen metaphor or sensory detail, like "as the sound of your foot on the stair/grows fainter."

Moore shows, doesn't tell. He serves up the poem to the reader and leaves it for contemplation, no reiteration of the main point, no pounding the idea through a final telling statement. His is the voice of a mature poet, one who truly trusts the image. He is not afraid of brevity, nor is he following contemporary literary fashion for fashion's sake: though he sometimes staggers disparate images in numbered sequences, the power of the poem mounting as the tension between the images builds, as in his poem "Love in the Ruins," he does not intentionally create fragmentation for its own sake.

Moore's work is fresh in its honesty and lack of pretention. The sensitivity of the poet lurks behind every poem, every artistically described moment. This book could only have been written by someone with a keen mind, an open heart, a moral sense, and photographic eyes that can see the invisible strings that connect us all.

CLOCK

Clocks which mark the passage of time from the cradle to the grave and are so intimately associated with the lives of men, are sometimes thought to have knowledge of what has happened, or is about to happen, in a house or a parish.

The first time I died, the clock stopped altogether. The hands whipped together like soldiers so that they seemed as one. The Roman numerals reorganized themselves into like shapes, the Vs with the Vs, the Is with the Is, the Xes with the Xes. There was no longer the tyranny of the circle. My life had ceased going clockwise, like a painted carousel pony. My life's white mane, white hindquarters, rusted bridle, faded hoofs, and the flaked paint of gold and green and violet feathered into the wind.

The second time I died, the clock merely slowed its infernal ticking, but in a highly irregular manner. Sometimes it would slow when it was thinking over the somewhat dingy facts of my life. Sometimes it would speed when it was pondering the net amount of good and ill that resulted from my thousands of insignificant decisions and the imperceptible outcomes from those decisions, arrived at through the most Byzantine of decision trees known only to the anonymous dendrites and suchlike caressing electrically the inner paths of my stiff, Baroque, clownish, mind, a mind that could fit into a small box, perhaps a match box.

This most recent time that I died, the clock began to chime and toll, though it had no such mechanisms within its humble, wall-bound person. With its non-sonorous clanging it carved a kind of hole in the air, a rectangle, a grave for all of the time hoarded and spent in my life, the curses and prizes, the occasional sights of the sea, the sounds of the wind through foxtail fields, the footpad of a stray cat, kind glances through doors and windows.

Matt Mauch

Notes taken in my grandmother's old metal lawn chair, like they don't make them anymore: on Lee Ann Roripaugh's *On the Cusp of a Dangerous Year* (Crab Orchard)

There are the choices we make that are clearly "ours." To go out with a spiked orange Mohawk. To get a tattoo of the Duluth life bridge, shoulder blade to shoulder blade. To runaway from home. To say "I do."

As well, there are the choices others make that become, de facto, ours, as in "Daughter/son, we're moving to Orlando," or "Your father and I don't love each other anymore," or "Harry, I just don't think, with the Internet, that we need a rep in the field."

Pause and look skyward to add your own examples. Don't worry about people watching you think.

Then be thankful for Lee Ann Roripaugh's *On the Cusp of a Dangerous Year*, which looks at the things you usually take for granted but see differently before or after you make or deal with a big decision that puts these things and the daily-ness of the life they represent at risk. What she provides is a kind of accounting, and to make this accounting, the poems connect the human world to the natural world. This connection, though, is not primarily to the natural world's wildness, i.e., to what we tend to think of first when we think of nature, but to the natural world's pedestrian qualities.

The "things" in Roripaugh's poems are often flying things that you'd find next to the mosquitoes and commercial jets on the spectrum of flying things, rather than over by the birds of paradise. We listen in as "one/ remaining cricket chirps resolutely/ into the night/ like an obsessive-compulsive's/ weird reed flute," and stare at "A fly who's been trapped/ in the sticky/ gum of flypaper—struggling, contorting/ itself into/ the twisted poses of a Mannerist/ painting, or as/ if it were playing a game of Twister."

Almost as often as the poems reintroduced us to flying things they reintroduce us to orb-like things and flowery things. The accountant-poet-who-is-on-the-verge-of-being-a-decider presents us with "an orange moon" that "wobbles in and out of the clouds, greasy/ and slick as egg yolk" and "the furred heft/ of a bumblebee repeatedly hurling itself deep/ into the dark purple heart of a tiny white/ pansy, which topples down and flops/ to the ground each time from the striped/ weight of the bee," as what the flying things share is their desire to both orbit and enter other realms.

The difference between accounting that would be merely accounting and accounting that is profound is reliant upon the intelligence of the observer paying the kind of very close attention that makes connection between things typically disconnected possible, i.e., the "cloud/ of tiny insects exploding against/ the brilliant heat of a street lamp. How courageous they are./ How bravely they/ blaze into ash in the bright yellow heart/ of their desire/ all night long while I go inside and wash/ my hair with your/ shampoo," and "maybe, like flowers, we must seduce/ pleasure the way/ butterflies are seduced into stopping/ for one moment/ to grip the round hips of buds and uncurl/ their tongue to drink."

It's impossible, I think, to read "the writhing muscular/ pulse of earthworms, their labia-colored/ bodies ribboned with a single blood-red band/ of color, their bobbing pale and vulnerably/ questioning heads" and be able to walk or look or hear outside after a summer rain teases these very same earthworms out to their deaths on concrete sidewalks without doing so differently.

As revelatory as these instances are, the real profundity of the connection doesn't occur in any one poem, but lurks behind the accumulating connections, such that the accounting isn't a list, but a path or stairway being constructed page by page. Which is how the poems seek, and the seeking leads to discoveries, and discovery, then, is what allows other of the poems to teach, oftentimes not because they have learned anything, but because they now can ask the right question.

This happens several times in several "human in the moment" poems that give the book, in the aggregate of these poems, the heft of character—of somebody building that path or those stairs in order to follow or climb or descend them. Somebody who after touching a silverfish notes that "it wriggled free, marked/ me with a faint pearled dusting of scales spangling/ the tip of my finger like the powdered glide of frosted/ eyeshadow," and wonders if "this is the same way you and I marked/ one another? Secretly and under cover of night?" and wonders further, summarily, "what can possibly come from all this tiresome spiraling?"

What we seem to be holding in our hands, in the final accounting, may have had a working title along the lines of *This Life Is Here to be Lived in the Moments You've Been Mistaking for Cracks to Spackle Over Field Guide to What You've Been Missing*. Thank the heavens for it. Now we, too, can hope to find things like a beetle we can hold to a book "like a small flashlight, so you can/ read by the bioluminescent spot on its thorax," and be or not be like two brontosaurs who "loomed up/ on the side of the deserted Nebraska interstate: life-size,/ garnished in gold Christmas twinkle lights, slender necks/ entwined, a red heart emblazoned above their heads . . . corny and improbable, oblivious to the fact/ of their own extinction," depending on how we answer the question, "how, exactly,/ should I have read these signs, if they were signs?" Rather than feeling like just another passenger, we can feel like something vital the next time we're coming in for landing, thinking of the airplane as "a clattering metal/ insect, the airport a hot neoned flower—cars tiny dark mites/ furiously inching along below in regimented swarms," thinking further "how insects can see ultraviolet, and how some flowers/ have petals tattooed with ultraviolet-reflecting honey guides/ to beacon the insects down into sweetness and gluttony."

And it's as if Roripaugh knows this—as if she knows that not only will we be different but she will be, too. Her intimacies are now ours. We become like the "tiny pale green nymphs" in the poem "Things That Are Filled With Grace," mistaking "my bedside lamp/ for the moon, swirling/ in clusters within the warm gold halo/ of light, then pausing/ to rest for a moment on the opened/ pages of my book/ like uneasily shifting hieroglyphs/ that cast strange shadows/ causing me to misread things," grace being a two-way street, and our accounting of it one of the few jobs we'll have for life.

Anna George Meek

A CELLIST DISCOVERS THE BODY (FROM MILL CITY MURDERS)

Minneapolis, 2010

This bright fall day, Anna Roble is compelled
to play a cello Bach Partita on the empty stage
at Orchestra Hall. She wants to be alone
but also to imagine people as vacant seats,
to feel the privacy around her
like the arms of a fantasy paramour.
She wants to hear the voices of the piece
weave throughout the hall,
calling to one another and yet somehow,
emanating from the same hollow body.

Intricate work, this delicate maneuver
of opening the stage lock, and already
inside her, the key of D major,
round and whole sounds: open,
honey-brown, the key of maple trees,
gold-filled canyons, key that staves off death
because the open strings could ring forever.
She feels her fingers selecting exact,
sweet places along the ebony fingerboard.
Tumblers in the steel doors click, and unlock.

Backstage, she lays her cello case open
like a child's coffin; she has her cello
firmly by the neck. She is pushing through
the doors on stage left, her eyes looking first
to the balconies, as always, keenly sweeping
the main floor and up to the skirt of the stage
to where the cellos' pins have pocked the floor.
That's when she sees the dead violist.

She looks at him carefully. She is moved
to tears, and she can see by his naked bloating
and the wet pillowcase twisted around his head,
his killer has not loved precision as she has.

Matt Mauch

Note taken in the three-season porch during one of the hospitable seasons: On Elisa Gabbert's *The French Exit* (Birds, LLC)

In one of the poems in Elisa Gabbert's excellent debut, a speaker still in love with a someone who no longer loves her back (for "the claim is 'Some bunny loves me.'/ It doesn't say unconditionally") turns (characteristically, we'll discover) curiously optimistic when she says, "If this were an elevator dream/ I'd suggest we hold our breath/ or our arms up maybe, make ourselves lighter." The optimism is curious because the speaker's no-bullshit intelligence and awareness is otherwise so keen. She knows a lot about a lot, and know she does, but doesn't flaunt it; instead, she humanizes it in moments where we recognize the part of ourselves that tries to shine a turd when a turd is all we've got.

As with a classically constructed novel, *The French Exit* is populated by settings, characters, conflicts, themes, and plots. In addition to airplane rides to the city where this year's party is, the speaker-protagonist takes us to cathedrals, libraries, fields, islands, and parks. In a cemetery, reminiscent of Berryman's Henry, we see that "Everybody's got the/ same epitaph anyway:/ Was Alive. Is Not. Tried/ To Save Life Thru Not/ Caring. Died Bored." After the protagonist's dream about playing tennis alternately with her brother and her ex, she sees, in a tennis game on television, that "they're showing footage from the courts and it seems like/ we're still out there: Man vs. Nature. I wonder out loud/ *if it's some kind of joke and one of them says If it is,/ it's the saddest, the longest, the slowest, most beautiful joke/ you could tell.*" During a cold-day walk along the ocean shore the protagonist comes across "This gull wing jutting up out of the sand" and wonders "Is there a bird down there, objecting? Politely?/ Excuse me, world. I wasn't ready to be buried."

In the way that a novel does—and what makes these

poems especially contemporary in the "life as it's lived now by those really living it now" sense of that word—these poems document and dissect (think formaldehyde, scalpel, frog) the struggles of living in our times, where, with a tinge of woe-is-me arrogance, we look at generations of long and not-so-long ago and conclude, "People were stupider then,/ less evolved than us because they didn't have to learn/ how to overcome cancer or master the joystick." Contemporary, too, is the hyper-deconstruction of our own awareness, where using a joystick becomes second nature, and we multitask, playing a game while realizing "yet,/ as far as we've come, technology still lags behind/ our desires." Where "The stink of the city/ grows worse, but at the same rate/ that we get used to it." Where "I would throw a game of solitaire" and "I remember as a child/ I always thought someone was watching me./ This was my earliest sense of the erotic."

The judgments rendered throughout tend to be informed by an aware fatalism, such as a beneficent agnostic would adopt—an agnostic who hopes that she'll find things out in this life if only she lives it well enough, who after another New Year's Eve celebration out of town, recovering the morning after, thinks how "Yesterday I watched the sun set/ from a plane. My past disappears/ like that, with grandiose fanfare/ out of proportion to the event." In another poem, taking in the clouds through the lens of Kakfa's diaries, we see our protagonist "sweep my arm through the air, and it leaves/ no trace, no neon zee," yet she says "I see continuous," despite which continuity, once "the moment's over" we "can't even/ save the stubs 'cause the tix've been/ digitized."

The poems create an ethical/moral system we don't recognize, but consider adopting because it makes all-caps SENSE. It's a system where laughter is "a kind of signaling/ that one gets it," it being the likes of friends who write "*You don't know/ how much you mean to me* . . . in a book,/ instead of telling me," which allows the protagonist to first observe that "Every time you reproduce a piece of art/ you remove some of its aura," which by deduction allows her to note "that's why/ your mix tape didn't impress me much," and then ponder "in the film/ version of the novelization of this poem [and I would up the ante to "this book"]/ I play myself but have fantastic breasts . . . my fangy tooth catches/ on my lip men everywhere crumple/ w/ the ecstasy and agony of it," such that the only sensible lesson from it all is "who needs aura in your movie when/ you're so hot it breaks people's knees."

In addition to the footsteps of Berryman leading up to this precipice that is Gabbert's *French Exit*, is the angel-dusted trail of Blake's pitting of innocence against experience, or, rather, an understanding of the pitting as a progression one works through, beginning in innocence, which one rejects for experience, from which one matures into a state of "organized experience," shedding the limitations of the earlier states of perception. The three parts of the book feel very much like a contemporary rendering of that progression. Part one gives us an innocent perception of despair. We see the protagonist projecting, "I keep thinking about a woman I met./ One day, approaching an intersection,/ she was afraid she wouldn't be able to stop walking," the protagonist making much ado, noting "I can see my pulse pounding right through the skin./ How minor can a heart attack be?/ Can you have one in your sleep and not die or even start?/ Just sleep right through it like a too-soft alarm?" In part two we see a kind of moving on, the state of experience mirroring the fact that each of the poems is a "BLOGPOEM," composed deliberately and in diary-like fashion, dispersed on the World Wide Web. We see a new but guarded confidence in a protagonist who says the morning chirping of birds is "the sound of their egos escaping from their bodies," who says a ride with death, after a drink with death, feels "like there's nothing more to lose than/ this week's top score on Pole Position." Then the third section presents us with a protagonist who isn't necessarily over despair, but is wiser as she incorporates despair into how she is living her life now, who sees/says, "I drive/ down the street and there is something/ under every leaf; each flutters independently/ as if to its own breeze" and "Sometimes the distance looks at me/ and for a moment I feel requited/ but then the distance rushes away/ at impossible speeds . . . it doesn't remember/ when we were touching, eye to eye."

To use Gabbert's own imagery, it's as if, in our journey through *The French Exit*, we start *in medias res*, all together on an elevator that jostles and jolts, such that images of all of us dying together fill our heads, so we mutually and instinctively, like a flock of birds evading a rock thrown into its midst, jump up in the air in the hope that doing so will lead to a soft landing. And then we land. And find the jolting elevator thing was just a glitch. And the doors open on our floor. And having thought seconds ago we were going to die, we exit both the elevator and that thought, and call it "living another day."

EMPTY NEXT SYNDROME

My husband awoke first and left our bed.

I pulled the blankets up, rolled over, noticed for the first time
that the far wall of our bedroom was no wall: it had always
been an entrance to a cave.

I can be pretty oblivious, I admonished myself while
wondering: how deep is this cave? How dark? I've lived here
so long, why have I never explored? Couldn't

I be an excellent spelunker? I remembered: sometimes
dangerous beings dwell
in the subterranean. I felt vulnerable

with only a quilt to protect me. Just at that moment

the stone walls of the cave began to writhe and swell, as if
they were flesh, as if baby feet were kicking inside a pregnant
woman's belly. A wolf emerged!

It stood perfectly still at the cave mouth. I was lying prone,
incapacitated
by horror. We stared at one another.

Then wolf pounced on top of me, its wet breath on my face.
It will tear my throat open! I thought.

Wolves tear people's throats open.

Our eyes locked on one another like a snake and its charmer.

Somehow, I wriggled out from under the blankets and from
under the wolf
and leapt to the bedroom door, never taking my eyes off the

animal.

I stood in the doorway, perfectly still.
It didn't occur to me to slam the door shut.

Maybe I couldn't; I don't know anymore.

"Jack! Jack! There is a wolf in the bedroom!"
My husband Jack appeared behind me.

He was holding a coffee mug, talking on the phone.
"Yes, that's a wolf," he observed and strolled away, continuing
his conversation.

That may sound indifferent, but it wasn't cruel, just
unthreatened. I had forgotten that I have always been the one
with the wolf/cave problem in this marriage.

I had no plan yet, except to stare at the creature, waiting for it
to murder me and "feast on my entrails."

Wolves feast on people's entrails; I've read about it.

At last, the stalemate ended: the wolf leapt at me! "You can
call him Killer!" howled a woman's voice from deep in the cave

but I didn't want to call it anything as it flew toward me.
Inches from my face, that wolf was yanked back

by a thick iron chain I hadn't noticed.
When it hit the floor, a loud thud of bone on wood. The prong
collar

must have hurt its neck. It shook off the fall and strained
toward me, never mind
the pain. I stood my ground. There remained a handful of
space the wolf couldn't

breach between us. Visually, I followed the chain far back into

the cave.
It ran umbilically through

the length of a narrow tunnel and back into a main cavern.
The space where the leash fastened should have been dank,
dripping

with shadow and mineral,
a primal, organic cathedral, but

it wasn't. The entire cavity had been renovated

into an upscale kitchen with marble countertops and bright,
high end track lighting.
So sterile in there, so right angled and harsh, straight out of a
magazine.

Had this space been co-opted because everything is co-opted
in this corporate world? Because it was underutilized by me?
Because I am suspicious of

overuse of the grotesque in art? For whatever reason, a well-
tailored executive
who had clearly overseen the renovation, and who had clearly
earlier

been the namer of the wolf, was leaning on a center island
giving some directions to an assistant. An assistant?

That cunt! I want this cave back how it was before
I remembered it existed! The wolf whimpered & strained. I
lurched

forward, arms open, and the animal slumped into my arms
with full trust,
I now understood it was being kept prisoner.

It had been starved.

I stroked its soft white fur, and I could feel
each frail rib beneath.

I felt like a midwife!
I knew I could liberate this beast!

First the wolf, then the cave. I began to scan
for tools to cut my animal loose.

Matt Mauch

Notes taken upstairs, in the room I'd call a parlor if it were downstairs: On Emily Pettit's *Goat in the Snow* (Birds, LLC)

It's a compliment taken from the high shelf when I say that Emily Pettit's *Goat in the Snow*, her first full-length collection, would've been a hell of a lot easier to blurb than it is to write about. Like a killer sunset, it's so damn much easier to appreciate it with assorted synonyms of "wow" than it is to describe to somebody else later on what was so cool about that particular half-hour before it got dark.

What "wow" means from this particular reader's easychair has to do with, in part, is how the speaker (henceforth synonymous, frequently, with "she") of these poems, throughout, displays both the audacity of the pre-socialized child and the insight *and* compassion of the old soul. She will approach the "you" of the poems saying, from the get-go, "Sometimes things get really beautiful really fast./ Good evening to you! Let's get nice right now," and in less than half a page will have shifted gears, saying, "Who needs to know why the airplanes go/ or the trees sway? I want to know why/ the weather changed when the door killed/ the cricket . . . why I'm not whispering this/ in your ear."

That persona, steadfast and pervasive, gets sprinkled like salt from the altruism shaker on a dish you're sharing with the sprinkler, who knows exactly how you like things to taste. The poems tend to begin with the speaker speaking as though she were reading the mind of the unidentified other. She says, "*Look above or below!/ It's a plant being mercilessly pummeled/ by small burning objects. Accurate blows/ to our best parts. What shall we call these/ places. Our best parts,*" and we feel like a seer has made what was muddy within us clearer. Then, after what strikes me as the bravery of 'fessing up to thinking that one can mind-read, the speaker, somehow comforted by such an admission, goes on to shares intimate things with the other. Without shame she acknowledges, "I am obsessed/ with an old problem and I have brand new/ megaphone. It is not a good thing. It is a most/ significant an ongoing mistake," and "Prominent cloud features are not far/ from my mind. It's an attempt to protect/ both of our mind circumferences from being mistaken/ for a shark that stops swimming. And other forms/ of disaster. I apologize. I would do anything/ for a different look from you." Finally, then, the poems welcome the other into the newness, into "If we develop a sufficiently powerful spacecraft/ for the purpose of exploring interstellar space/ will our minds succeed in growing sufficiently/ elastic to survive the travel? . . . There is a chance that the elasticity/ we want will be ours. All there is, is a chance./ And everyone know chances are strange./ And sometimes chances are like planets/ that get too close to their stars."

The lost art of the as-welcoming-as-it-is-uplifting-one-sided-conversation, bastardized as it's been by paid motivational speakers, self-help gurus, et al., is found here. The speaker professes as a classical capital P Professor in the movies might, but the well she draws from is atypical. The knowledge she imparts (with the requisite theatricality that keeps the audience at the edge of its seats), comes not from reading or doing, but is the kind of professing from the kind of professor who remembers every dream she's ever had, dreams she uses to govern her days, Ph.D. of So-Called Sleeping. "Try to remember where you last leaned," she says, "where you last left no trace. Here is a tiny elephant./ Put it in your pocket and it can be the elephant in the room," and "You say, *I'm watching you.* And I say, *No, I'm watching you.*/ I am the government on the moon and/ I mean to let you forgive me."

Though it may well be a dazzling mind we're witnessing at work in these poems, what matters is that it's also a dazzled one. As if impossibly occupying both ends of a teeter-totter, She Who Governs Her Life By Her Dreams is self-balanced by She Who Anchors Herself In This World With Anchors That Form Patterns, and patterns, we all know, are things from which we're hard-wired to extract meaning. Some of the anchors are elemental: fire, snow, and their compatriots. Other of the anchors animal: elephant, giraffe, fish, bird. Up the ladder are the more abstract anchors: gravity, space. And the meaning/s of the pattern? That, I think, is found in the two anchors that appear most often—science and brain— anchors that operate as terminals wherein the stuff of this world and the stuff of the other world court each other, and what's ultimately so alluring here is the activity within those terminals, disembodied takes on the bodied life. Struck like people-watchers are struck, we logically equate the artifact that we call "poem" with "the steam that rises from the boiled mind." These aren't the poems of a poet channeling a muse; these are the poems of a poet filtering original perceptions through all of the tangible and intangible things that make up "her," filtering them up and out, as if the she's reached an ecstatic state and is literally boiling over. The result doesn't have a name that I know of, but if it did the definition of that name would be "the opposite of cliché," as in "The problem is solved. We etch-a-sketch/ the problem being solved. It's pretty/ complicated looking. It looks like a duck,/ until we shake it. And when we shake it,/ it looks like a new stranger, a fancy glance,/ too many telephone poles/ a twitching mind" and "the orange is on the edge. And I am/ on the edge. And later I will repeat, *I am/ on the edge.* The edge is both the point/ at which something is likely to begin/ and end. This is the astonishing power/ of generosity!"

Goat in the Snow presents itself, via the titles of most of the poems in it, as a HOW TO manual. We're schooled with "HOW TO RECOGNIZE WHEN YOU HAVE BEHAVED BADLY AND BEHAVE BETTER," "HOW TO STOP LAUGHING WHEN YOU LAUGH AT INAPPROPRIATE TIMES," "HOW TO APPEAR NORMAL IN FRONT OF YOUR ENEMY OR COMPETITOR," "HOW TO KNOW THE WORTH OF WHAT," etc. Almost immediately, we identify with or actually become the unidentified other addressed by the speaker. And what I, in that role, keep finding or constructing as I read through these poems is the narrative beneath the veneer each poem is glued to. I read "A goat is not a sheep, though I know people/ who have made this

mistake not meaning/ to be flippant" and then on-its-heels
"This is not how to start a fire/ with sticks" and the story
line that occurs between those two (seemingly) associative
lines appears to me like a daydream. And while it's impossible
that anybody else out there is supplying the same narrative,
that impossibility is exactly what I'm convinced is occurring
from sea to shining sea. It's like being infected by some kind
of lurking narrative; you find yourself robotically under the
influence, supplying footnote after footnote to fill in the
space between each hop, leap, and launch. What this does
is stitch the reader and his or her life literally into the poem
on the page, i.e., it brings the poem *off* the page in the same
way you take the points of stars in the sky and carry them
around as constellations complete with not only with their
communally shared mythologies but also with their personal
significances—the night at X you did Y with Z under a
reclining Orion. Wow.

Sharon Chmielarz

BURNING

"...I don't want to be burned."
Louise Glück, "Averno"

Ah, but, I want to burn, the way the field, the strong field,

the known field is burned in fall and spring in anticipation,

oh, much quicker than the slow clearing of flesh from bone.

Burned, loose from its scaffolding, flesh is a change into light,

into motes, scattering, over field, dust, catching in air, once

every winter I see this play as snow descends on a field

and its field tree, gloriosa et immaculata, and the joy

watching that change, I stand in the field by myself. At home.

You had children, I had none, I have no one to show the field,

or tell I'm sorry, or call and ask if they are lonely,

I have something to give nothing; call me a show-off, call me

willing to cut off my nose...when it comes, I'm ready to burn,

free of all boxing or packaging, it won't last long, that heat, that

singing intensity on the flesh and then, the vibrant exit into wind.

Matt Mauch

Notes taken from the tool bench the previous owner left in the basement, which I've converted into a bar, so now he haunts the place: On Lauren Shapiro's *Yo-Yo Logic* (New Michigan Press)

The poems that open this ever-opening little book present moments when the mind, prepared for a kind of fantasy, because it's imagined it, is out and about in the world, in a body, when preparation meets opportunity: the figurative ménage a trios happens. The student painter painting the figure model imagines that "The world is reflected/ in the belly of the nude that shows me only/ an ever-repeating image of myself . . . hunched in a ball/ in the belly of the nude woman." Then the tryst occurs. The painted woman "wants lunch./ We eat the still life next to her./ I can't even get into what happens next." But what happens next, and next after that, matters. Getting everything you could ever imagine you could want has its wages. The student painter hangs her painting in a show, where neither she nor the man standing next to her know what to say about it: "It's colorful, he says./ Thanks, I say."

The prepared mind/poet continues to have this streak of luck—all these figurative trysts—but continues to continue the story after the tryst, when the mind is still in the body in the everyday world. Seems there was a curtain behind the curtain we choose—one that we somehow missed seeing— and now it gets pulled back, and the poet feels obliged to tell the reading public, *It's not all it's cracked up to be.*

As if surprised to have entered a new stage of life, the poet of "THEY PROMISED ME A THOUSAND YEARS OF PEACE" lets us know, "The snow falls blank as a contract no one/ will sign . . . When I lick my shadow/ it tastes like the ground and vice versa . . . Getting back to zero is awesome/ if you're coming from negative numbers." It's the kind of recognition that leads first to stasis, which grows to paralysis, which blossoms as a kind of performance. Only it's not the poet dressing up for the show, but the poet dressing up the world. Sure, the poet says, "When I bite into the apple, it tastes like an apple./ Like most inanimate things you see/ before you touch: unsurprising," and sure, too, but also, "Making statements of absolutes is like drinking cocoa:/ meaningless but comforting./ Step away from the dotted red line!"

From this poetic game of dress-up, then, comes not a regression to but a resurrection of true truths of that seem to come from a childhood if not exactly our own childhood (next curtain, please). "The Rubix cube," the poet determines, "is only as hard as the pasting on/ the colored squares wants it to be," and "Being dopey can be endearing/ but only to those who already love you," as if, for all of us, like Stafford's old deer-pusher, the poet pulls back the curtain behind which there are no more, only a wall, and on that wall is writ, "Later people would speak of the times as *the times* and bow their heads like cattle," and we're looking into a mirror. *We* be the people.

The fantasy, it becoming fact, the letdown, the letdown's postpartum, the making due with, the reclamation of: it's when you can sally forth as an aggregate of it all, like a nesting doll that knows exactly what it's made of because it dissected itself and then put itself together again, that the chances for real intimacy present themselves. "Come on, Kathy says," to the poet, to us, "can't you just enjoy it for once? By now we know/ who patented the steam engine,/ but think of all the men who tinkered around,/ helping to invent it," such that the only logic is the illogic of the yo-yo, which doesn't sound illogical at all when "it's so cold it does feel like something huge is about to happen," when we see "our features slipping off our faces," and with an affirmative so-what "go home anyway and make love/ and rub our blank faces together," feeling "a deep/ and exciting newness welling up."

Jim Coppoc

EULOGY

Michael, they found you
weeks too late, like a bad
tv detective show, by
the smell and the mail
overflowing, your dogs
starving, standing by you,
your ferrets gone savage
in the house, your cat
resurfacing days later
from an unknown
secret place

I hear you had become
300 pounds, had stopped
shaving, had grown your
hair long in the style
of the Levites

I hear you stopped
paying the electricity
and water, began
a garden, abandoned
it for the sake of meditation

Michael, they say you are dead,
your chanting no longer
incessant. They say your golden
robes are tatters, your serenity
shattered, your eyeballs bulging,
unable to close.

Michael, you are dead, but I am
unable to touch the body. Your
casket is closed, your family
is weeping, your house is empty

It is not yet real, this.

RITUAL

I wake up with the sun,
and we are the same
age: seven. It's my birthday,
and my mother is happy. We make
chocolate chip pancakes and sing a song
about me. We twirl in yellow dresses and I
hold her hand—she wears me like a bracelet.
Outside, we have no shadows, there are
no bees, no clouds, no mud puddles, only
a seven year-old sun that doesn't hurt
our eyes. We pick flowers that don't die.
She waves her wand-arm and they grow back.
I open presents in the grass, all from her.
Later, we share an ice cream, cuddle, kiss,
she plays with my hair, smells my skin. She
further softens into my purple blanket, and we
never check
under my bed. She isn't there.

Matt Mauch

Notes taken in the garage, neglecting rather than engaging the project on sawhorses: On Stacia M. Fleegal's *Anatomy of a Shape-Shifter* (WordTech)

Shape-shifting sounds cool in theory, when it's a comic-book superpower you get from a radioactive mosquito bite, but when it's everyday shape-shifting, and the impetus to be something other than what you are comes from the circumstances and family you were born into, having to do it becomes something to fear, less superpower than tragic flaw. When the female killdeer that "feigns a broken wing" in order to lure potential predators from her egg-filled nest becomes a model for the speaker in the poem "Decoys," it comes at the human cost of awareness. The poet-speaker builds a nest just like the killdeer, only around "a rocky place," not a nest, and it comes with the caveat "as if my predators/ won't know" and the caveat portends "As if we can/ truly mask fear, or trade/ one for another."

The shape-shifter here concludes via action that shape-shifting itself isn't about wearing masks so much as it's about inhabiting identities. The speaker moves "forward into fit,/ bathing in the first/ lip-parted second of this merge—/ having bathed first/ in the flush of want,/ and now the sheen of having." It's a having that occurs in moments rather than with any duration (aside from the simulated duration of moment after moment after moment in a chain). "*Spend each beat as if it were/ your first,*" declares the speaker, in mimicry again, this time of "the hummingbird's fervor" to "be not just energetic, but energy" so that one can "endure/ the heartbreak of a thousand flowers a day."

Often, the identity entered into is sexual and dominant, even when seeming on the surface to be passive or mutual. The other does what the other does while the speaker points out "the neck's that swivels it into place, makes it all/

possible, is the starting point of/ the body-wide undulation desire pulls/ from hot breath, stretching it into a long sigh." The speaker "counts sun rays on your jeaned thighs/ in time with the thrum of the wheel at my right ear" and notes "it is still/ me trusting you, in your hand or my mouth,/ still me bending away from red road signs." Again and again the speaker is "open/ to the chance that submission to your-/ self is not like submission to another."

These body-to-body connections are not without their downside. Each moment of connection has embedded in it not only the little death when the moment ends, but also the awareness of the coming, post-crescendo drop-off. "Press your face to this/ like my thighs are cold, like you could shatter/ me," the speaker says, but reminds "I built this box, remember? . . . it's my choice, just as it would be if I bent/ to fog a series of ohs with my own mouth/ to blur what you think is yours—what I invent." Clearly the speaker is aware of as much, although the other is never in on the secret, if we can call it that, behind the necessity to shape-shift. "The master's house is covered in cobwebs," the speaker says, "He thinks I've brought a broom."

She so defiantly embraces the moment as end-all be-all, and when intimately connected body to body is still alone, that the eventuality of her *really* being alone, and embracing solitude and self, comes not as a surprise but as the only possibly satisfying conclusion. This leads to examination of the shape she'd assumed: "I wonder if/ love is just a burnt synapse, a brief lapse/ into excessive serotonin," she says, and "Where did o-f fold back to make f-o to meet r?—/ *of the body's* only part of the diptych, *for the body/* enjambs."

This isn't deconstruction, but reconstruction of that which is unabashedly female. "I swallow a birth control pill the size of an egg—," after which our speaker tell us she gags, but is "safe another day, so long as it works,/disables me." It seems, in fact, that the only vulnerabilities our speaker admits to are those that come with gender. It's the only part of her world, being first a girl and then a woman, where she entertains perspective in the form of been-there, done-that advice. A grandmotherly figure, "wrinkled as a century-old oak/ but twelve-hundred rings stronger" scolds as much as she advises when she says, "*I didn't walk out on my abusive husband/ while pregnant during the Depression/ so you would one day be submissive to cruel men!*" And while the spirit of the advice provides the speaker with an island of hope, men aren't the people she has trouble with.

"When he touches me,/ or I sing, my mother is/ defied," the speaker says, and therein lies the rub. We don't shape-shift just because; we shape-shape due to the amalgamation of failures to live up to not only expectations but standards of simple decency. The end result is felt young, "I said bitch. I said my mommy is a bitch./ I said please. I throw up on the carpet," and resonates when one is no longer young: "it was easy to toss me/ aside,/ the parenting experiment/ that failed." Whether the multitudinous connections which replace alienation, embracing the self as a function of the body, are "healthy" or redemptive we never know. What we do is that when eventually the daughter grows to look like the mother, she has no choice but to ask, "(Am I you?)," and given who she's become, no choice but to answer, "What is true/ is that our many old selves/ fit inside the other . . . each scooped out deeper than the one before,/ so holding more."

PILLOW TALK

Laryngeal prominence: bulge with a bible name, when gulping
that forbidden fruit, did something get caught in your throat?

Appalled, I watch it move, smaller than the mouse who travels
up and down from our basement and simpler to crush under my boot.

Too much of your internal plumbing pokes through your skin.
What a mess this leaves you in, exposed with every swallow.

Apple of discord, sharply defining our differences, like a saddle
in a steady trot. Who fares best? Which is fairest? What is not?

I hum, temple and cheekbone pocketed in your shoulder. Soon
your voice bobbles in, whirring through its windy knob.

Don't imagine your deformities attract me. I prefer unobstructed
esophagi. Still – the profile of your throat – it builds

range into my view: an alien mountaintop, a familiar little hill.

Matt Ryan

SHE AND HE AND THEY RIDING A GONDOLA IN THE SEWER

We find ourselves getting married in the sewer, because praise God, holy hallelujah, it's cheap down here, costing so much less than a Valentine's card. The people up there send us messages from their flushed toilets linking capitalism to love, using the first quadrant of a Cartesian plane to prove this nexus.

For those of us who don't look for the SEC to approve our mergers, this is where we are—hiding underneath the slam of angry manholes. The people up there affix pheromones on the feathers of a dart, now that their bulls, blinded by plucked-out eyes, prefer green to red. The people up there don't know what the people down here know: Cocoa trees grow best in the dark.

The people up there fund these sexy scientific projects so that diet soda can harpoon a whale, sperm or otherwise. Invest in your future, they say. Meanwhile, their nurses lament: There are no babies in the hospital. These women in white, with no one to guard, use charcoal to light their tears, an offering that smells of a waste that can't be wiped from the floor of what used to be a honeymoon suite but now is the lobby of a funeral home.

These kids down here, this man and woman, this man and man, this woman and woman, lover and lover, wear wedding attire patched together from electric blankets, waiting to donate their nakedness to each other—the heat from their nostrils proving that warmth comes from gross places, which is basically what our cats taught us: Love means you'll lick an ass clean.

Matt Mauch

Notes taken in the side yard, where I've replaced the grass with rocks, pavers, and such, so I can take better notes there: On Aimee Nezhukumatathil's *Lucky Fish* (Tupelo Press)

Weaving your way through the different poems in *Lucky Fish* is like being the new boyfriend or girlfriend at the family gathering, being introduced to everone, and this isn't a run-of-the-mill family. Neither dysfunctional in the way that so many turned-into-literature families are, nor perfect in a way that the black-sheep poet can never hope to measure up to, the family here is like a finders-keepers roll of hundred dollar bills on the sidewalk—unexpected as hell, and pretty damn awesome, peopled not only by the flesh-and-blood relatives, but just as tangibly by the family's beliefs, stories, legends, superstitions, hopes, and ghosts.

"When someone is burned to death, find a crispy calculus/ from that spot," says our family-guide/speaker, and then "Let the spirit of the crawling stone shake/ your pocket. You will be so rich." This is a family with not only a history, but a mythology that actively influences their lives. A psychiatrist mother who overhears at work "a woman threatening to hang herself with a bra" brings worry home to "two girls, hungry for a bedtime/ story," yet raises them, ages, and "Now she clutches a rake in my garden./ What new hope does she scrape in those beds?" A father who smuggles fruit-tree seeds into the country in his shoes commands the attention of a 15-year-old daughter who admittedly knows nothing of patience at the time, thinking, "All I wanted/ was to go inside into our cooled house and watch TV/ or paint my nails," when he points out "galaxies/ or Andromeda or the Seven sisters" as she's being eaten alive by mosquitoes. The result of such rearing is the gift of being able to see that "The frog who wanted to see the sea was mostly disappointed. He preferred/

wing-dance and jump on soft mud fen. No salt to sear his tender thin skin./ Sometimes it is better to say home, stay put."

In the same way that "Some/ believe the turtle carries the whole weight/ of the world," the family mythology is entwined with the beasts and birds and rocks and soil and plants that make up a diorama wherein "everything/ comes to life, even the sand tamped/ down with glue shimmers. Every/ wispy curtain seems to blow aside,/ revealing a spectacular sun." It's no surprise that the family-guide/speaker wants "that turtle to put down/ his pack tonight and join me at the table." Clearly, it's her turn. "Out of all/ these tiny green islands, there/ is only one where you and I/ could not think about going/ back to work," our family-guide/speaker notes, choosing instead to "think of a tiger shell/ rubbed shiny from worrying it/ with my thumb, and sometimes, when we see/ a metal spoon or candlestick wash ashore/ we'll think of our other life, our past life—/ a world of meaty stews and snow." She knows and tells of "a man who has such a sweet face,/ bees follow him down the street. Ants still collect/ in the tread of his shoes" and points out that "Your laughter scarred the butterflies into flying like violets, little notes of/ alphabets & grace. Who invented the alphabet of snakes & worms? Prophets/ that face each day on their bellies?"

It feels very much as if our guide through this natural and supernatural family history is the one outside observers would peg to be the heir to the matriarchy—is indeed herself one of those prophets she's musing about. That would explain like nothing else I can think of such pointings of the way as "There is no mystery on water/ greater than the absence of rust./ The very lack of it only moves/ each reed and shorebird to bend./ The question is a blanket/ for yours shoulders when you/ finally reach the shore./ The question is a rope/ so it doesn't float away" or "The wishes of sand are simple: to slip soft under a tumbling of shells. A slide/ into the happy mouth of an oyster. To get stuck & rub into you like/ an angry letter. Or sometimes soft as a kiss" or "The white square stone found inside an eel's head. Dry it, and roll it/ in your hand. Can you hear the tinny music of the bone? Beetles/ you have never seen before will wind their legs in protest." You want to follow this one.

And the beat goes on, literally. The family-guide speaker gives

birth, making the end of this mythology the beginning of a
new chapter in the same. In a social-media era that allows
for the rampant over-reporting on the goings-on of one's
children, what's so very, very refreshing —and I say this as a
childless adult—is how transcendent the mother-son poems
here are; none of the banalities stacked upon banalities
hidden within the sort of "a silly thing happened while potty
training today" reportage that makes you hide mothers
who can't tell quirky and cute from Shinola® on Facebook
appears. Instead we get the post-birth "When I hold him in
the sunshine/ even his ears/ glow from behind like a church
window shining/ a celebration within" and "Without/ my
glasses, the edge of his foot blurs even more/ during those
early morning hours until is shimmers/ into a perfect peach
sold by my favorite fruit farm/ on Route 20 where the old
lady who shuffles out/ to measure my haul of fruit is still
in her flowered/ nightgown, still in her slippers" and the
laid-bare pre/during birth admission in the long "BIRTH
GEOGRAPHIC" that "My three-page/ single-space birth plan
shrank/ into one sentence—'Mother alive,/ baby alive.' And
when my husband wasn't looking, I snipped it/ to just two
words:/ Baby alive."

The third-person mother-son poems late in the book
subtly acknowledge, like an agreeing nod, that the gift of
the poet-speaker's family is a gift not only to her son but,
through this book, to all of us. "There are only about five
hundred whopping cranes/ left on this planet, three hundred
California condors,/ and just over six thousand or so beach
mice," the speaker of "WAITING FOR HIM TO SPEAK" says
as she does just that, noting "By the time/ you get to the end
of this poem, there will be no more/ pygmy rabbits on earth.
The last one will die/ as she waits for her son to speak," which
is neither matter-of-fact nor woe-is-us, but instead frames
the urgency of the gift being given. The poet/speaker/family
guide tells us that she is a "lucky fish," a slippery talisman
that we are glad to have, but without our daily attention will
go belly up. A gift like this—what I'd call a real one—requires
as much as it bestows.

Paul D. Dickinson

I LIKE THE WAY YOU TILT YOUR HEAD

I like the way you tilt your head
It is a tiny gesture, really
But it means the world to me
And I'd like to get inside there
To do a little dance
Inside your skull
To show you all the reasons
Why
I should be your only one
But if men understood women
And women understood men
There would be no rock n roll
There would be no poetry
And there would be little use
For messed up guys like me
But there I go again
Off the deep end
When I could of just as easily said
I like the way you tilt your head

Joyce Sutphen

AT THE TRUTH BAR

The men sit with their dogs on their laps
and their wives at their side. Man and wife,
man and dog—they resemble one another.

No one has anything to prove; they order
baked apples and whipped cream; they
drink beer.   It is winter and raining—

They had almost forgotten about home,
but now it comes back to them as they
gaze over the dark Mediterranean.

The Salsa band is bored with the little
crowd—but they are brothers and have
their own private jokes. After a while

they are playing rock and roll,
which is when I think of my aunts and uncles
and how they have always gathered in places

like this, arriving early to find a table
big enough so they can see each other
all around, so they can get up and dance.

Matt Mauch

Notes taken on napkins in various locales, as if I were a traveling circus: On Lauren Ireland's *Sorry It's So Small* (Factory Hollow Press)

"Wasps don't sting they bite," says the speaker coming to her own conclusion, damn it, in the not-as-defiant-as-it-is-revelatory "THE SUMMER OF TWO THOUSAND FINE." Unwilling to accept received knowledge or perceptions at face value, this is a speaker who in six lines that the extra white space between words makes feel like twelve or thirteen—like what you're getting here is two for one or more—goes from "I'm gutted" to "Actually I have seen my dad cry" to "Everything/ I remember about three is wrong" to "Give me my fuckin money," emerging page by page of this fantastically illustrated letterpress chapbook (and I've not included the white spaces in the lines I quote just because it would be so hard to do justice to, so you'll have to buy the book to see what I mean) as a big-R Romantic hero with equal parts Byron and Keats, only in the body of woman living when we do.

"Being lonely is extravagant," our hero says, "like sick home from work," sick and tired like "the birch tree only on fire with thoughts," thoughts that have no purchase in a world where "it's raining . . . but the sound-man is not making sounds." It is a world where others, more often than not, disappoint, as if they aren't strong enough to endure life on this plateau. This leads to resentment. "I really wanted to delight you with my collections," our speaker says, and "I intend to punch you with my ring," and "I am hating you from very far away." But out of resentment, despair, etc., as if out of some sort of fertile-if-you-can-get-past-the-smell manure, the hero's grandiosity blooms. "If the future is a roller rink my skates are white/ and my smile is white & I am dead & I am/ couples skating to Cypress Hill," she says, and "Did you know crushed beetles make good lipstick./ I have

fallen in love with a beetle" and "I-beams sway to comfort
me./ All of Poland has turned out to hold my hands./ Gently
weeping wolves. The tender hare."

In the Romantic hero, old and new, is both rebellion
and embrace, and each of those comes in pedestrian and
transcendent flavors. It's what makes the hero complex,
simultaneously, from our bleacher seats, pitiable and to-die-
for. We aren't surprised to see our hero embrace workday
drug use. It comes with the territory, as does the hero's
candid celebration of the same. "I get high and listen to the
music of the spheres . . .," she says, and "When I am drunk
I am so pretty . . ." Such off-the-cuff celebration, though,
is only half the story. Following the afore-typed ellipses,
respectively, are ". . . I resent the full stop" and ". . . like my
best friend," making the seemingly workaday something
done in the name of the name of the otherwordly and
out-of-body—so much more complex and interesting and
enviable. Lest we settle, though, on her path as a path we
might similarly tread, she reminds us why she's the hero here
(and why we're not), saying,"I'm not on drugs/ or anything,
but I can see the molecules vibrate./ Plus there is a cheese
sandwich inside me, making me feel cozy."

These aren't emotions recollected in tranquility; they're
emotions captured the moment they flame up, just before
(reviewer clears throat) they consume that which they were
nourished by. The hero notes not only that "We are reclining
in our own ways in front of/unbeautiful men" but also says
"The dirty window can keep my goddamned face." This is a
hero dwelling where the Romantic hero dwells, in the throes
of, such that the poems are a kind of anatomy of "Maybe you
think you've been here before feeling and doing things like
this but I am here now and this is a live unedited report." And
it's true, we identify with her. We have asked or wanted to
ask, "Would you like me better if I had brown eyes." We have
said or wanted to say, "Let's make out in your mother's car."
We, too, would like to go back in time to "beat the shit out of
my former self." We have been there when "the night is/ put
out & the rain/if it is coming/ doesn't come."

And our hero of record, she identifies with us, too,

although that's a dynamic we wouldn't toss into the "happily ever after" bin, not when "I fucked your right through the dream catcher" is counterbalanced by "You move through the tunnels of me/ you are the toasted odor of decay." Not when the dreamily and seems-rhetorical "Is there anything sadder than taillights" has no accompanying question mark, just a period and a one-word, next sentence "No." But that's who are Romanic heroes are, and we will live vicariously in their memoirs of "disappointment & glitter, disappointment & glitter/ love stuff love stuff blah blah blah," no matter how small they claim themselves to be.

AN UNCERTAIN PRAYER

after Anna Kamienska

God let me forget the definition
of *kinematics*. Allow me

the power to change
nearly nothing. Make the world

completely ignorant
to the many sufferings

of tiny spiders
and let large waves

continually wreck
like falling sheets of porcelain.

Make your voice unheard
and lift your love off us

like a burning blanket.
Allow us the unclenching

of hands. God let me
no longer take up space

and let the space I free up
be a poem.

Gretchen Marquette

THE SECRET

Once, I watched a man
toss the weighted stems
of false flowers
toward the opposite bank
of a filthy river. From time
to time they stuck, waving
for a moment
before becoming still
and this pleased him.

Until now, I've kept it quiet,
where to find the brightest,
most exacting love.
Much of it burns off,
but is no less real
than the plate of pink

frosted cookies, the red
baby in the blanket they wouldn't
let you touch, a memory
they tell you
you were too young
to have made.

What remains, remains.

Sometimes I suffer
for love, being fox wild
and desire a trap.
Body intact,
I recognize the places
I've slept, despite every

branch broken
and the new snow.
What I said before,
about love –
I meant that sometimes
you have to let it be.

I've never told anyone,
but often I walk around
thinking only of the hollow
of a throat or curve
of a shoulder and sometimes
I hold the reins of horses
who are men, in hiding.

Once, we sat under hot light,
round room plush with the breath
of strangers. I said, *We have
fifty pages left to love one another*,
and across his chest burst a sash
of gold chrysanthemum.

One thing I've learned –
you have to let love be a practice,
for what might happen

elsewhere.

Matt Mauch

Notes taken in the kitchen, in the chair I'll vacate if the cat decides she wants it: On Ed Bok Lee's *Whorled* (Coffee House Press)

Almost as if it's a chemical equation, Ed Bok Lee's *Whorled* seeks what lies on the other side of the = sign when the verb of its title is paired with its homonym (whorled + world), sucking you into where, whether or not you know it, you already are. Next to you now, though, is the poet as tour guide . . . with an agenda. In a world that seems so different from earlier versions of itself, where occupy movements pitting the 99 percent against the 1 percent only scratch the multifaceted surface of our long cold winter of disconnection, this is a poet-speaker-tour-guide seeking, and finding, unities.

There are unities with the lives and worlds brought like satchels by parents into the new-world lives of their children, unities with the meaning-making plots and characters of legend and myth, unities of circumstance and place that are the experience of the immigrant, and even unities of spirit that feel like connecting with past lives. "Can you hear it?" the poet asks, "Wind in iron jars buried inside the living:/ Grandmothers, past spouses, cable men, priests." And alone near the sea "our/ sleeping shadows/ stealthily remove a single marionette/ from the moon."

These unities of the worldly and otherwordly are propelled along by unities of language. When the grammar at hand isn't sufficient for forward movement, the poet invents a construction that is. In "Night Work," where one feels nestled within a dream within in a city within love, the poet speaker's "mother's death/ protect-fills my love with sadness," and he wonders whether it's his mitochondria that "powder-sugars the moon." In many of the poems, there simply aren't any periods as all, as if the reader is being given the choice to walk through the door the poet is holding open, or to stay put.

Without contraries, of course, is no progression. The unities in *Whorled* stand next to that which opposes them, like a saddled lion trailing a saddled lamb in perpetuity on a carousel. At the casino, we see "the somber Crip with a queen diamond/ and six spade tattooed on his neck, his plaintive chant:/ *every minute is a worse-possible hand*," and "the young mechanic/ who hits the Super Bond 007 jackpot/ but wasn't of legal age to collect." The poet encounters a bag lady at a zoo who "wore Prada, couture, & one torn nylon/ the other naked shin banana-blue-black . . . surrounded by the suffocation of moldy fur," and he wants to "give a dollar yet not offend." Like love that ends for who-knows-why yet stays with us like a shadow, the failure to unite or stay united after knowing unity leads to a sad strain of hope.

In *Whorled*, it's participating in this kind of sadness that makes refugees of all us. Whether the wars we flee are the wars of the gambler, the wars of culture, the forgotten war-war of Korea, or out-of-sight/out-of-mind war-war of Iraq, the plight of the seeker of unity is universal. The poet takes us on an odyssey of such seekers, encountering Circes, Sirens, Scyllas, et al. We go from a Lower East Side party where "you impersonate a fire/ to transmelodica as the year turns blue" to a casino where the poet sees "Tolstoy . . . dragging your oxygen tank to and from the Wild Sevens slot island/ three nights in a row before they stretchered you out" to a Russian steppe where "a Tatar warrior steadies his mare, lights/ a joint, and ponders/ all the little sails racing/ to and from the eyes of strangers" to a bowl of dog stew in Korea where "Maybe you'd rather not/ have another serving,/ but eventually you/ can get used to it" to "Those grunts in Iraq/ who stuck that steamy/ mutton twat/ then offed her parents." "What did anyone expect" the poet asks, then segues into the long poem "If in America," where, via the second person point of view, we are taken on a tour of the mind of the shaman Hmong hunter who in the confusion of being accosted by a group of white hunters acts on a lifetime of preparation that speaks in the voice of an instinct that says "if a gook/ don't be dumb one," asking "Would *you* set your rifle down;/ hope the right, the decent,/ the fair thing on this buried American soil/ will happen?"

A jokbo, we learn, is a Korean family tree of sorts—the record of a family bloodline, in the poet-speaker's case going back seven centuries. As the odyssey ends and the unities begin to come through this poet-speaker, rather than existing independently in the world out there, it feels as if what we're holding is a new kind of jokbo for a new kind of world where history can no longer simply repeat with a new costume on, but must make itself anew because the old first rules no longer apply, as if History itself had parents who had died, and now it has to figure out how to move forward without them. The poet, post-journey, is matched now to the task of translating the unities of a new world, and is accepting of the newness itself, such that gratitude becomes a higher order unity. "*A new empire will of course arise,*" the poet channels, "*until then, perhaps there is work down in/ this city below.*" The paradox itself is acknowledged: "I'm happy," the poet-speaker says, "This method is unfailingly, always just barely enough." And that method? That happiness? "You want to write about the universe," the poet says, "how the stars are really tiny palpitating ancestor hearts/ watching over us/ and instead what you get on the page/ is that car crash on Fourth and Broadway—/ the wails of the girlfriend or widow,/ her long lamentation so sensuous/ in terrible harmony with sirens in the distance."

The prophet-poet of *Whorled* makes a kind of elegy for everything—an everything that includes all of us now and next. "Dear speaker in a future age," the prophet-poet says, "when only a handful of lexical bouquets/ remain to light these monstrous highways/ I write this to you as a human/ piece of coal," and not only a piece of coal, but a piece of coal with the earned vision to see that "yes, that Broadway car crash was fucked up,/ but the way the rain fell to wash away the blood/ not ten minutes after the ambulance left/ was gorgeous."

Steve Healey

REWARD SYSTEM

I'd walk a mile for a Camel.
Moreover, said Thoreau, you must walk
like a camel. With four crooked legs,
therefore, I'd walk a crooked mile
across an Egyptian desert. I'd saunter like
a furry comma through the Mall of America,
elevating my heart-rate for twenty minutes.
I'd haul my humps all the way to Glocca Morra
if at the finish line a tasty factory-made cigarette
waited for me to smoke it. In addition,
it is said that Jesus once said that it's easier
for a camel to pass through the eye
of a needle than for a crooked man
to enter the kingdom of Glocca Morra.
How are things in Glocca Morra?
How do camels get so small if they are
in fact quite large? It is said that they store water
in their humps, but that's not true.
Over time they have adapted to being
without water and cigarettes for long journeys.
Their kidneys and intestines, for example,
are very efficient at retaining water—their urine
comes out as thick syrup, and their feces
are so dry that they can fuel fires.
It is said that from those fires camels
can light their Camels. Furthermore,
according to Thoreau, camels are the only beasts
who can ruminate while walking. They eat
then regurgitate what they eat then chew
what they regurgitate to enjoy it once again,
all the while walking a mile through
their crooked thoughts. Camels,
in other words, make thoughtful vehicles,
and according to Jesus, they are the only

beast to have replaced the wheel
where the wheel had already been established
prior to the twentieth century invention
of the internal combustion engine.
When they cross the finish line they can finally
swallow that cud with one good swallow—
then it's time for a Camel and an Ativan,
maybe even a fortune cookie.
I'd walk a mile for a fortune that says
it's time not to walk another crooked mile.
For the truth is, things in Glocca Morra
are not looking very bright, and now
it's time to walk a mile into the fires
of the twenty-first century.

G.E. Patterson

BRIGHTNESS BEGINS

for HX and for NC

Whatever it is you think you are feeling
In time   what may be a real source of this
Lies in your senses   so you disbelieve
We were ever on our way to a place
Where the love we dreamed could carry us
Into the past where the first hurt might be
Seen and then forgiven   so many times
We never imagined   brightness   begins
Here perhaps for more than ourselves   in shadow
There is a place shaped like a home   in shadows
No one would miss   indeed   no one would long for
Years without feeling   shadow and relief
Form   so that form will not be a surprise
        Now   somewhere around here   let it begin

Dean Young

MY FRIEND DOBBY

If Dobby Gibson contracted a veneral disease,
it was from Venus herself.
A Dobby it is called, the painful grit
in the corner of the eye while skin-diving
as well as cheating on the miniature golf scorecard.
The technical becomes less and less believable.
At the center of the mind is a high-speed chase
while you hold an enormous bunny against your chest.
Your heart and the bunny are trying to agree
not to kill each other. It's silly to expect
the government to work any better than that.
I may be a little drunk. Dobby's CD collection —
I recommend touching a cobra instead.
Dobby Gibson, Dobby Gibson is the shout
that goes out over the bug-lit summer lawns
making all pine for a carefree childhood that never was.
Never was, Never was is the cry that goes out
and comes back in like the yo-yo waves.
When Dobby was a child there were no other children
thus he never learned to skip and still thinks
a lollipop is a sexual position (see above).
Yes, he fell asleep on the observatory's roof.
Yes, he hid in a shower stall while whatshername
knocked and knocked (see above). When Dobby
ate the heart of the Aztec, he gazed about
for the next human sacrifice. Botticelli
laid down his brush, it can't be done he admitted,
i.e. representing Dobby. Sure it can, said
unnamable outer space phenomena. How much electricity
is too much to expect from a single outlet?
Even by the graves we are covered with herbaceous matter.
Life is everywhere! How difficult to feel nothing,
says the doctor. The thing I love most about
the desert is every rock has a face. What I love

about Dobby is the snapped-off music-box ballerina
he tenders in even his most acetylenic brawls.

What they call acknowledgments, I call these people/places/things rock

The institutions, organizations, and individuals that made the second annual Great Twin Cities Poetry Read feel like a springtime potluck of poetry are, in no particular order:

The AFA in Creative Writing Program at Normandale Community College

The Pocket Lab Reading Series

Lowbrow Press

Water~Stone Review

The BFA/MFA Programs at Hamline University

Graywolf Press

Coffee House Press

Rain Taxi Review of Books

The Twin Cities Literary Calendar

Paper Darts

Whistling Shade Press

MSU Mankato Creative Writing Program

·

Matt Ryan
Dobby Gibson
Jeff Peterson
Matt Rasmussen

Please give them your thanks and your business.

Signed, The Management

www.ingramcontent.com/pod-product-compliance
Lightning Source LLC
Chambersburg PA
CBHW051834090426
42736CB00011B/1807